**FOREST**

*Tide*

Manisha Sobhrajani has lived and worked in the wild, untamed mangrove forests of the Sunderbans as a full-time volunteer with the Samarpan Foundation. She also travels to Jammu & Kashmir to work with groups of women on issues of trauma-healing and reconciliation. Her book *The Land I Dream Of: The Story of Kashmir's Women* is a gripping tale of the lives and times of Kashmir. She now lives in Goa.

*Also by the same author*

The Land I Dream Of: The Story of Kashmir's Women

# FOREST OF

## The Untold Story of the
# SUNDERBANS

### MANISHA SOBHRAJANI

hachette
INDIA

First published in 2018 by Hachette India
(Registered name: Hachette Book Publishing India Pvt. Ltd)
An Hachette UK company
www.hachetteindia.com

1

ISBN 978-93-5195-019-6

Hachette Book Publishing India Pvt. Ltd
4th/5th Floors, Corporate Centre,
Sector 44, Gurugram 122003, India

Typeset in Dante MT Std 11.5/16.9
by InoSoft Systems Noida

Printed and bound in India by
Manipal Technologies Limited, Manipal

Because of Patrick,
and
for Dia, Mallika and Hitesh

# CONTENTS

# BEAUTEOUS FORESTS OF TRYSTING RIVERS

Eighteen coiled serpents guard a harvest of hundred-two eggs
Sometimes, hungry, they eat their infants
These are salty ever-thirsty rivers, hungry for the sweetness of earth
Hungry for its forests, animals, birds, humans
For its trees, flowers, fruits, its honey and mahua

What they nurture, the rivers seek to devour
Where the eighteen rivers swamp the ocean
It's difficult to tell sweet from salt, sift life from death
The goddess of trysting rivers heals with her breath

Rivers, like lovers, enter and leave these lands at will –
Absent travellers who rock the anchored earth

Defined by water, the definition of land keeps shifting
The grammar of tides keeps meaning on its toes

The tiger is ever present, seldom seen
The honey belongs to the bees, and to my Bon Bibi
The mangroves watch the land from water
They bare their roots, but bear no fruit
Mudskippers peep through wet earth, letting it breathe
A lavender lotus soaks in the sun, garlanded by a water snake

Another, promiscuously pink, reigns the pond
Hermit crabs outgrow their shells, find newer homes
A black goat shrugs off a persistent swallow
A kingfisher bluer than blue has seen something new
In the tender sun, a bird gleams black-blue like the night
A boat turned upside down is being painted black
A kid goat tries to stand on its wobbly feet

You think the tide that sneaked in last night
Sleeps this morning, tired of the tryst
But the tide's in the humidity of your breath
It's in the tongue that moistens my lips

*(Being an account of what I think I saw with Manisha in Bali, next to Gosaba, one of the hundred-two islands that form the Sunderbans, on 14 January 2015)*

S. Anand

# PREFACE

Sunderbans: where the river rushes to meet land for six hours a day, until, like a jealous lover, the sea claims it for the next six. Known as much for the rise and fall of tides as for its mangrove forests, it is a land where the eager moon sometimes appears at 4 p.m., and where, on a clear night, the seven sisters of the Pleiades seem surprisingly within reach. Where, as the sun rises and sets, it presents vivid oranges, fiery reds, passionate purples and vibrant pinks across the sky and water.

It is a land where people grow paddy, potatoes and mustard on their modest patches of clayey soil – an exercise that requires intense labour and time – and survive on the produce for the entire year. The lack of water for irrigational purposes does not allow for much agriculture, and growing a second round of crops in the same year is not possible for everyone. Families that can arrange for irrigational water are able to plant a second crop, but most cannot afford it. The only water naturally available is brackish, which combined with argillaceous earth, does not make for an ideal cultivation scenario. From the time the seeds are sown, in June–July, until the time paddy is harvested, in November–December, every waking hour of the locals is spent looking after the crop, like one looks after a precious commodity. The rest of the year is spent toiling equally hard, fighting the severe monsoon and the intense winter – preparing for their arrival and then dealing with the repercussions. Peppered in between is a never-ending saga of combating attacks from snakes, crocodiles, forest animals, cyclones and floods. Since it is inevitable that the local people have to venture into the forest – to collect wood, honey and other resources – such encounters are unavoidable. And though the natural phenomenon of cyclones and floods is a matter of routine, their onslaught is still alarming, unsettling and damaging.

One wonders how the early settlers in the Sunderbans dealt with these catastrophes. The recorded history of the Sunderbans begins from as early as the 5th century BCE and there are reports that suggest habitation in this wilderness began in the 3rd century BCE. Towards the end of 2013, fishermen from the small hamlet of Gobardhanpur chanced upon terracotta artefacts and fossilized bones from which experts have concluded that human settlements could have existed in Gobardhanpur and its vicinity as early as the 3rd century BCE. They seem to have lasted till 3 CE and after a gap, the relics indicate a new civilization from 7 CE onwards.[1]

The modern history of Sunderbans begins after the British set foot on Indian soil in the 18th century. The Sunderbans was marred by tribal invasions and, later, by the Battle of Plassey (1757), both of which were aimed at possession of land. The Partition of the Indian subcontinent, first into India and Pakistan, and further into Pakistan and Bangladesh (East Pakistan), played more havoc. This caused serious damage to Mother Nature, and eventually resulted in the division of the Sunderbans – with all its shifting water bodies and land masses – into the Indian side and the Bangladesh side, with 102 islands falling within Indian territory.

In 1963 and 1971, refugees from East Pakistan poured into India. Taking the cue from the practices of the British Raj, the then-government 'accommodated' the refugees by encouraging them to raze the trees in the Reserved Forests in places like Jharkhali and the Herobhanga islands and grow crops.[2] It is, therefore, no wonder that the region has a diverse and thriving culture, an amalgamation of beliefs and traditions practised for the safe-keeping of man, beast and property. People of all traditional faiths, including the tribals, have their own belief systems here that are determined by the natural world that surrounds them and their survival in it.

It is here in the Sunderbans that the goddess of the forests, Bon Bibi, resides: protecting those who seek her grace. Of the many miracles she is said to have performed, the most spectacular remains the one where she brings Hindus and Muslims together and reinforces the universal message of a single godhead. Manasa Devi, the Hindu goddess of snakes, is worshipped in this wilderness for the prevention and cure of snakebites as well as prosperity and fertility. She is denied a full godhead due to her mixed parentage for though she is Shiva's daughter, it is the snakes who raised her. Manasa Devi is kind to her devotees but harsh to those who refuse to worship her. Dakshin Rai, the deified tiger, rules over the beasts and demons. He is feared and respected. While Bon Bibi protects the people of the Sunderbans from him, she is also said to have taken Dakshin Rai under her wing. The demarcation between enemy and friend is vague here, as is the distinction between land and water.

This is the land of eighteen tides: *athhero bhatir desh.* Yet, even today, to get a pitcher of drinking water, one must walk several miles. Electricity is a rare phenomenon and depends on how benevolent various NGOs working in the area feel towards a particular village on a particular island. As for medical infrastructure, the area boasts of a single government hospital. Quacks abound, like ducks in tiny, man-made ponds, in almost every house.

Public transport usually means a motorized cycle-rickshaw van – the kind used in cities to sell vegetables – and one-rupee rides on a passenger ferry to take one across the river. Of course, if one wants to go to a different island, it is a matter of combining a van and boat trip, both of which are time-consuming and tedious, but this is accepted as a part of everyday life. The other option – a rather expensive and futile one – is to hire a private launch that offers comfort, space and food, depending on how much one is willing to spend. But when the tide is low, the launch can only go up to a point beyond which one has to disembark and either take a smaller boat, or wade through slush to get to the shore. Also, even at high tide a launch can go right up to the shore only when there is a jetty available, which is not always the case.

In the Sunderbans, one wakes up to a cheerful dawn heralded by the calling of the brain-fever cuckoo as early as 4 a.m.: the name of the bird itself suggests dementia. A walk around any village means the exchange of greetings, sharing of the local gossip, mulling over everyday affairs while exchanging home-grown goodies like *tetul* (tamarind), sweet potato and pumpkins, fresh cheeku and coconut from the trees and, of course, fish, crabs and prawns – the day's catch from the river – if one has been lucky enough. At night, snakes, spiders and scorpions give you company while mudskippers, crabs and hermit crabs ensure there is never a dull moment during the day. A sudden swarming of bees – like a dark cloud that moves too quickly – means a queen bee has hatched and left her current hive with some of her workers in tow to start a new hive. Depending on what hour of the day and tide it is, the mangroves and their associates display the most intricate and interesting network of gnarled and twisted roots, creating an image of the limbs of a horrid witch cooking a potent mixture of poisonous herbs in her cauldron.

Although mobile phones are not a novelty here and service providers' networks are reliable, meetings are not fixed over phones; rather, a message goes around by word of mouth, through several messengers, in the midst of lush, green paddy fields – a network quite like the roots of the mangroves. The locals are as used to living in their unpretentious mud huts as in a boat for days at a stretch. They cook, eat, bathe and sleep, in what may appear to city-dwellers like myself as 'limited space'.

William Blake's *Songs of Innocence and Experience* may well have been set here: the mystery and magic of the natural world in contrast to the ruthless reality of everyday affairs; myth and folklore co-existing with the chores necessary for daily survival. It is to this mystical wonderland that the Universe sent me in early 2013.

# INTRODUCTION

—

## ARRIVAL

In 2008, I went through a life-altering experience. A car accident resulted in my husband's untimely demise. My six-year-old daughter, Mallika, became wheelchair-bound. I sustained multiple fractures and damaged organs. We were both confined to our respective hospital beds for nearly two months. Our discharge from the hospital was followed by the death of my father. It was then that the Universe introduced us to the rather intangible concepts of 'faith' and 'healing'.

It started with my coming in contact with the Samarpan Foundation, a charitable trust that provides assistance of any kind where there is a humanitarian, ecological or environmental need. People associated with the Foundation are ordinary folks who have experienced the vagaries of life, and thereby, have come together voluntarily to assist others who need support. Mallika and I have received immense love and acceptance from the Foundation which helped us heal. We have been able to accept and live a different way of life as a result of realizing that the acumen of the Universe is all-knowing; therefore, all that comes our way is within our capacity. Having recovered psychologically and emotionally, Mallika resumed school, while continuing to be wheelchair-bound. I offered my time to work on projects undertaken by the Foundation, which is how I found myself in the Sunderbans.

In May 2009, cyclone Aila had struck the eastern coast of India and Bangladesh. The widespread destruction it caused made the Sunderbans a household name. The water levels stood as high as 9 feet on land and took several days to recede. Rescue and relief operations from outside the Sunderbans did not reach until four days after the cyclone had hit. The magnitude of loss – of human life, vegetation, especially the mangroves, wildlife, domestic animals and goods – dawned on people as well as the state and central governments of both countries alike over a prolonged period of time.

The Foundation sent its volunteers for immediate relief and rescue operations and their involvement and intervention has continued in the Sunderbans ever since. As soon as it was possible to work in the region, the lack of availability of potable water was addressed by facilitating the digging of tube wells on several islands. Medical teams made weekly visits to these islands, on motor-powered boats, to attend to people's primary healthcare needs.

By this time, it was clear that the Foundation's intervention in the Sunderbans would be long-term. Thus, a large piece of land was purchased to build a campus out of which the various activities of the Foundation would be carried out. Bali, the second-largest island, was chosen for establishing a base, purely for practical reasons – it was relatively easier to approach than some of the other islands. Transportation of goods, especially construction material, would be easier to Bali because of its proximity to the mainland. Land was readily available for purchase there. A spacious house was built foremost on the acquired land. The purpose was to provide a comfortable set-up for the Foundation's volunteers who would come to work in the Sunderbans.

In 2013, the Foundation decided to construct a charitable hospital. Creating a medical base at Bali would address the basic medical needs of approximately 95,000 locals from Bali and its surrounding islands. The assignment was offered to me and I accepted. I knew that it would be a Herculean task to co-ordinate and supervise the construction of a hospital in this remote, poverty-stricken area where even basic amenities like drinking water and electricity were precious commodities.

The word 'Sunderbans' promptly brought to my mind two things – the cyclone Aila and Amitav Ghosh's book, *The Hungry Tide*. I re-read the book in an attempt to get a feel of the lay of the land. I was hoping to make the most of this opportunity for introspection and contemplation, something which was near impossible in a city.

I arrived in Kolkata, from Goa, with a mixed bag of emotions. The Foundation's volunteers in Kolkata had organized my travel from the airport to Bali, or Balir Dweep, as the locals call it. After locating the taxi hired for me, I embarked upon a three-hour journey by road through small industrial towns and picturesque villages, to arrive at Godkhali, the riverfront which proudly displayed a board that read 'Gateway to the Sunderbans'. The next task was to find a man called Swapan, who, I was told, would be waiting for me at the Godkhali jetty with his boat to take me to Bali.

The path leading to the jetty was lined with small kiosks selling tea and different kinds of savouries; some were selling basic items of clothing, even utensils. Here began my first attempt at speaking Bangla: 'Swapan-da *kothaay*? (Where is Swapan-da?)' Many enquiries and a few phone calls later, it was apparent that I wasn't going to Bali in Swapan-da's boat. For someone who was familiar with the surroundings and set-up, it would not have been a difficult task to find another boat. For the uninitiated, however, it was not as straightforward as it seemed. As I enquired in broken Bangla, and a mix of Hindi and English, about the various ways in which one could travel to Bali, dusk was approaching. It was evident to the shopkeepers that I was a newcomer to the area; what they could not believe was that I could be so naive! They explained that while one could hop on to a passenger boat and then take a cycle-rickshaw van, it was too late in the day to exercise that option. Hiring a small boat at the time of *jwaar*, or high tide, was foolhardy. The only option therefore was to hire a bigger, cylinder-powered launch.

By now, the 'how' and 'what' no longer mattered. The shopkeepers were kind enough to take matters out of my hands and into theirs. They spoke amongst themselves, summoned boat owners, haggled over prices and 'fixed' a launch for me. I was told I was lucky that it was high tide and, therefore, possible to bring the launch right up to the jetty from where it was currently anchored. This would not have been possible had it been *bhaata*, or low tide. The exhaustion of the day meant that I did not process much of what was happening around me. After a wait of about half-an-hour, by which time I calculated I had been at Godkhali for close to an hour and a half, I was informed that my launch was ready for me. A bare-chested man, most likely in his early twenties, clad in a lungi which was folded upwards from his knees and tucked in at the waist, took possession of my bags. I assumed he was my launch driver, Subroto. Without further ado, I thanked the shopkeepers and followed him. The jetty was partly immersed. The rhythm of the tidal waves and the darkness around made me dizzy and I was grateful for Subroto's steady grip on my wrist as he helped me onto the launch. I found out later that Swapan-da had misheard the time of my arrival and had returned to Bali after waiting for me for a long time.

I took in my surroundings as I settled on board while the powerful engines of the launch set it into motion. The Gosaba river stretched towards the horizon, an occasional twinkling of diminutive lights visible on either side of it. What I assumed to be fireflies were, in fact, solar-powered lamps lighting up huts along the *baandh* or embankments of villages we crossed on our way. The *baandh* was lined with mangroves. The foliage was so thick in places that it was impossible to fathom that something lay beyond. It gave the impression of travelling through darkness to enter a forest of tides. This, and the cool breeze from the water, along with an oversized half-moon hanging overhead, made everything seem surreal. Approximately an hour later, Subroto announced that we were approaching the Samarpan Foundation jetty on Bali.

By now my eyes had become accustomed to the darkness. As I was disembarking I saw two men waiting, sent to welcome me and collect my luggage. After having travelled almost the entire day, I was glad to set foot on the concrete jetty. The men – Binod and Guru – led the way, with torches in hand to guide us on what seemed to be a mud track lined with mangrove trees. We walked the short distance of about 300 metres to reach what was to be my 'home'. From having felt dismay and anxiety earlier in the journey, I was now feeling curious and excited. As I reached the threshold of the Samarpan Foundation campus, the fragrance of *rajanigandha* flowers, or tuberoses, engulfed me.

Based on what I had read about the Sunderbans, I had conjured up an image of living in a mud hut with a thatched roof woven with palm leaves. When Binod and Guru led me to a *pucca* infrastructure on the campus, I was pleasantly surprised to realize that not only did I have the privacy of a bedroom, I even had the luxury of an attached bathroom fitted with a shower!

The Sunderbans is one of the remotest places I have lived in. Life there moved at its own pace and the nature of daily events took over my existence. Initially, the lack of 'creature comforts' was a novelty that I almost enjoyed. As I got more and more involved with the project, the novelty began to wear off. It bothered me that the closest bookshop or café was five hours away; that if I were in an emergency situation, it would be a while before help could arrive; that the village panchayat had the capacity to pose a security threat to my daughter and I; that a cyclone was unpredictable and could disrupt and damage everything.

I did not maintain a diary or keep notes about the incidents that took place; they were simply registered in my subconscious. During my stay in the forest of tides, there was little else I could think of or do other than the project. Living and working on the project site was therapeutic initially as it helped me keep my focus away from the events of the previous years of my life. But after a while, the remoteness took its toll, and loneliness struck home. It seemed as if I were wrapped in a bubble and this life that I was living was not real. But when I returned home to mainland, almost two years later, city life seemed harsh and senseless. I missed the wilderness; it bothered me that I now had to worry about paying bills and making ends meet. In brief, the stark contrast between living in the Sunderbans and then coming back to live 'normally' was not easy to adapt to. Writing about it later was cathartic; it helped put things in perspective and analyze them from a distance.

The sequence of events in this book is not linear; that was never intended. I chose to write about what influenced me the most, and it did not necessarily follow a pattern or chronology. I allowed myself to be guided by the same force that led the rivers to meander and dictated the lay of the land.

In this book, I have shared with the readers my lived experiences, and have also tried to give them a glimpse of what life is like for the local people living in the Sunderbans. The sequence of events in the book may slightly differ from how things actually unfolded during my stay there, but the essence remains the same. As far as possible, I have used the real names of people who walked along with me in this journey.

I had moved to Bijaynagar, Bali Island, Sunderbans, and this was going to be both home and workplace for quite some time. The Foundation's campus was located on the periphery of Bijaynagar village on the banks of the Bidya river and was surrounded on the other three sides by fields. At the farthest end of each field was a small hut owned by the family who nurtured the fields. As the day commenced, women and men went about with their respective tasks, while the children reared the family cattle first, and later went to school, which was easily a walk of half-an-hour, if not more, from their homes. In the afternoon, when the sun was at its hottest, the village went into hibernation for a couple of hours. Late afternoons and early evenings suddenly brought about a fresh burst of energy and everyone came together in a collective effort to keep the fields thriving.

We were going to construct the hospital building with a new technology: polyethylene terephthalate (PET) bottles filled with sand were going to be used instead of contemporary mud or clay bricks. Steel rods and bars were to be replaced by fishnet. This had been tried and tested previously in an experiment where a small room was constructed in New Delhi to check the viability of such a construction. The experiment had proved successful. Later, the technology was tested at the Structural Engineering Research Centre (SERC), Chennai. After the appropriate certification, it was declared that plastic bottles and fishnet were suitable for construction.

We hired locals to work at the construction site, some of whose lives have been recounted in this book. Before work commenced on the hospital and jetty sites, we stocked up on construction material: bags of cement, sand, stone chips as well as bricks and steel rods, since the construction of the new jetty was to be done using conventional methods and materials. When it was time to replenish the stocks, we ordered a fresh supply. This was when I learnt that patience was to be one of the most crucial lessons I would take away from the Sunderbans. After three days of waiting for fresh construction material, I pressed the panic button. Endless phone calls to two different suppliers simply brought promises and reassurances, but not the material. It was frustrating to see the work slow down and eventually be brought to a halt for two whole days.

In a city, one could simply pick up the phone, place an order for the material required, sit back and be assured that it would be delivered to one's doorstep. In the Sunderbans, however, it was a different story altogether. After the order was placed, first the supplier himself would have to procure it from the closest town which stocked construction material. Loading it on trucks and sending it to Godkhali, the riverfront, was the next step. Thereafter, it was a fresh journey – the material had to be off-loaded from the truck and loaded on a boat, locally known as a *bhotbhoti*, echoing the sound of its engine, that was used for ferrying material. This was done by a group of labourers, called *muthias*, at Godkhali, who had formed a union. They worked on their own terms and conditions, whims and fancies, and, of course, in rhythm with the tides. Once the boat carrying the material reached our jetty, a similar set of *muthias* in Bijaynagar had to be given the contract for off-loading it and delivering it to the Foundation's construction site. In other words, one had to keep a margin of at least ten days between the time the material was ordered and supplied.

After the first setback to work, due to lack of construction material, I learnt to plan ahead. I ensured that we always ordered for fresh stock well in advance.

From the time of my arrival, until the time I left Sunderbans, the forest of tides – that is, from 2013 to 2015 – the story of my life intertwined with that of the Sunderbans. Much like the coils of the serpentine rivers that meander around the islands, I often lost my way and then found myself all over again. It was an unusual life, without roads or electricity, yet as normal as anywhere else, with many 'heroes' – wonderful women and men of integrity and strength of character who worked with me – as well as 'villains' who tried to disrupt the work on the project. While there was the apparent purpose to my stay at Balir Dweep – building the hospital – this was also, quite serendipitously, a perfect setting to harmonize with nature and heal and mend from the untoward incidents of the previous years. It is this story that I would like to share with my readers.

I have divided the book into four sections – Land, Water, Mangroves and Horizon. The first section introduces the reader to the way of life in the Sunderbans, as I discovered it. The tough living conditions, the absence of basic amenities and the humility and grace of the local people. Even though the forests pose a grave threat to the people, it is upon these very forests that they depend for their livelihood. The land has a fascinating history – of its coming about, and its occupation by humans; being mistreated as a bountiful natural resource to eventually becoming a wildlife reserve. The possibility of it becoming a Utopia, with its own currency, was almost certain at one point. But Mother Nature had other plans.

The second section, 'Water', delves into the mythology

and folk tales associated with the land of eighteen tides. As fascinating as these stories are, they also remind us of the power of nature. These very rivers threaten to run over village embankments, destroying cultivable land. The pull of the water also poses a continuous challenge to concrete structures like jetties, which, in a place as remote as the Sunderbans, are like lifelines. The rivers swallow up land as well. News of islands shifting, or completely submerging, was alarming to me, but not to the locals. It brought home the message of impermanence and of the transient nature of almost everything.

'Mangroves' explores the livelihood options for the locals, which are mainly forest-based. This section narrates the legend of Dukhe, a young boy who goes into the forests, comes under imminent danger, and is delivered from it by the omnipresent Bon Bibi. This, to me, profoundly reinforces the dependence of the locals on the forests. It also explains their reverence towards it.

'Horizon' takes a leap: from the Foundation's project-in-the-making to a project functional in its nascent stages. It also explores, very briefly, the impending threats to the Sunderbans: the setting up of coal plants, economic development, the inevitability of climate change and its effect on the mangroves, and eventually the fishing trade. The locals worship the forests and its beasts; yet, they venture inside and gather its resources to make ends meet. Therefore, the man-animal conflict is as natural to the Sunderbans as is its water. Despite the threats and the dangers, the people of the mangrove forest love their land and will not leave it.

While each of the sections deals with various stages of the hospital project, it simultaneously gives a glimpse of the way of life in the Sunderbans, the way the locals live it. It also displays how outsiders are made to realize this very fact: that they are outsiders.

I was living in the forest of tides now. Quite like petrichor, the earthy fragrance that accompanies the first rain shower, Bon Bibi's being had filled mine. The more I found out about her, the more intrigued I was. As I was about to commence work on the hospital project, I invoked Bon Bibi, and sought her protection and divine guidance to take me through the adventure called the Sunderbans.

# Land

—

## The Sunderbans Way of Life

A lone heron struggled to find a safe perch, flapping its wings helplessly against the strong winds that were threatening to blow away trees, uproot mangroves, capsize boats and destroy everything that came in their way. People ran helter-skelter, unsure whether they should try to save the humble thatch-roofs of their tiny houses, the meagre goods they owned, or their paddy and potatoes, which they needed for survival for the rest of the year.

But the wind and the rain seemed determined to destroy everything. I was cooped up in my room, in an unfamiliar place, unable to decide what sounded more dangerous: the eerie wind as it howled through the village, the crash of a falling tree, the hull of a boat dashing against the concrete and steel of the jetty, or the collective sounds of panic emanating from birds, beasts and humans alike. It was unlike anything I had ever experienced. Perhaps this was nature's not-so-subtle way of initiating me into the Sunderbans.

After almost three hours, the wind and rain finally abated. The cyclone had ravaged everything in its wake. The rice fields and huts were damaged; the mangroves were uprooted, causing the embankment that encircled and protected the village to break down at places; cracks had appeared along the ground as a result of which the tidal waters were seeping into the village through the many breaches. Water – a source of life – had, yet again, destroyed the lives that people here so carefully tried to maintain.

The morning after the cyclone – only three days after I had arrived in the Sunderbans, in January 2013 – I was at the jetty, standing on brackish silt, where the blue of the sky, the green of the mangroves, and the muddy, brown waters of the Bidya river stretched as far as the eye could see. The cyclone had left in its wake contrastingly serene weather. A solitary boat on the river added to the tranquillity of the landscape. Coming down from Godkhali, where the Gosaba and Bidya rivers meet, on the left bank was the island of Gosaba and on the right bank was the island of Bali. The two were united in the destruction that the cyclone, or *ghurnijhar*, had caused, but the damage was little in comparison to that caused by the cyclone Aila. I was to later realize that cyclones of such small intensity were aplenty. They did not even get named unless they were as large in magnitude and as destructive as Aila.

Subsequently, each time I stood there, the vastness of the river filled me with a sense of awe and reverence. The landscape took on myriad shades, particularly during the immensely beautiful sunrises and sunsets, when their hues became more intense, as if nature was ruminating on the richness of life. It was surreal to witness this natural, ethereal glory.

The jetty that I stood on was hardly a year old, and already it showed signs of being worn down by the seasons and storms it had witnessed. It had two platforms and a few steps to aid movement during the changing water levels. During low tide most of the structure was visible while during high tide everything except the upper platform was submerged. The force of the tides pulled and pushed the solid concrete in opposite directions, resulting in cracks.

No amount of reading or research could have prepared me for a life in this forest of mangroves and tides where everything was governed by *jwaar* and *bhaata*: the arrival and departure of boats; the time of day when fishing commenced and people went into the forest to collect firewood; work along the embankment, either for repairs or for building new boats; or making fishing nets and even a visit to a bank!

Behind the jetty were paddy and sweet potato fields at different stages of growth. Beyond that stretched the village of Bijaynagar, where there were no roads, as with everywhere else in the Sunderbans, barring the island of Gosaba. The popular mode of transportation was boats, or walking. Later, I would find out that carts powered by motorized engines were also used to transport people.

Each day, I grew accustomed to a life of no frills, yet one that remained as mellifluous as the waves. Initially, I marvelled at how people lived without electricity. Later, I got used to it. I considered myself lucky if there was sufficient charge in the solar-powered battery to charge my phone and laptop, and if the ceiling fan functioned at least for half the night! Such thoughts faded away as I realized there were more pressing needs that had to be addressed, such as clean water and basic medical facilities. The locals – born into hardship and having minimal interaction with the world beyond the Sunderbans – accept life and all its trying situations with immense grace and humility.

Walking around the village in the aftermath of the cyclone, I could see people repairing their homes. Later in the day, I ensured that the roof of my dwelling was anchored to the ground with aluminium wires to prevent it from being blown away. This was to save me from being roofless in the subsequent cyclones, of which there were at least five during my two-year stay at Bali.

The locals viewed me as a strange young woman who had come to live with them on the island. While some greeted me politely, most were curious and yet suspicious about my motives. Why would a single woman leave behind city life and choose to live in a remote village on an island in the Bay of Bengal, surrounded by mangrove forests? The shopkeeper who sold me the aluminium wire did not hesitate to let me know that the delta was no place for a woman who was not born here; that I should return home after some sightseeing.

Walking around the village of Bijaynagar one evening, I came upon melodious voices raised in song. Drawn by the sounds, I entered a small hut where three men were praising god Krishna:

*Janama saphala ta'ra, Krishna darasana ya'ra*
*Bhagye hoeichey ek bara*
*Bikasiya hrin-nayana kari Krishna darasana*
*Chade jiva chitera bikara*

(One's birth is successful if, by some stroke of luck, one can have Krishna's darshan even once.

By seeing Krishna through the openness of one's heart, one can view the world through a new consciousness.)

7

They welcomed me with smiles, and the lady of the house offered me a chair. Sensing my interest, they sang with more vigour. I was moved to tears. On finishing the bhajan, they encouraged me to join them the following evening and promised to teach me how to sing . This warm welcome was perhaps the first that I had received since my arrival at Bali.

However, I couldn't go back to them for a long time. Exploring and acclimatizing myself was demanding. I had to learn about the landscape and how to navigate it. Moreover, the hospital project had to be set into motion.

The literal translation of the words *sunder ban* in Bengali language is 'beautiful forest'. It is said that the region of Sunderbans derives its name from the Sundari tree, the mangrove species *Heritiera fomes*, that grows abundant in the delta. The wood of the Sundari tree is very tough, and is used for building houses, boats and furniture. There are many theories relating to the etymology of the name, however. One suggests that the word *samudraban,* or 'sea forest', morphed into 'Sunderban' over time. The name could also have been derived from the name of a primitive tribe named *Chandra-bandhe* that inhabited the area. The story goes that a wealthy and influential merchant, Chand Sadagar, built a massive city that spread across the delta, and that the name of the tribe originated from him.

Spread across India and Bangladesh, the Sunderbans is at the deltaic confluence of the largest rivers in the Indian subcontinent: the Brahmaputra, Ganga and Meghna, the last flowing entirely through Bangladesh. What was once an extensive, thick forest has slowly given way to human population and its need for agricultural and habitable land, and wood for fire and fuel. Of course, this has been at the cost of the extinction of some species of flora and fauna. The forest, or what remains of it now, still acts as a guard against storms and cyclones. It is an ecologist's paradise, where land and sea meet to create unique life-forms, like the lung-skipper fish, which is able to breathe both on land and in water. 'The descent of the dinosaurs 65 million years ago coincided with the ascent of one of our planet's most hardy plants – mangroves. In the magical, inter-tidal universe of the Sunderbans, it is still possible to see "cusp" life forms taking sustenance from both land and sea.'[1]

Fifty million or so years ago, the formation of the Indian subcontinent and, simultaneously, of the Himalayas, was underway. Violent yet slow tectonic movements were shaping the planet. The Tethys Sea, which rimmed the northern part of the subcontinent where the Himalayas now stand, disappeared as the Indian plate collided against the Eurasian plate and literally squeezed the land upwards. From this emerging mountain range, tonnes of silt from the Tethys Sea kept getting deposited to form what would become the largest delta in the world. Eventually, this land mass rose above sea level, forming nascent deltaic plains. Changes in the sea level then caused severe flooding in the Bengal region. Drastic geographic changes in the newly formed deltaic plains that took place approximately 10 million years ago eventually resulted in the delta as it is today. But the mangroves had already been here for at least 50 million years before the delta was formed.

The current region known as the Sunderbans, however, has a recent history of human settlement. The Ganga–Brahmaputra delta became secluded from the receding sea around 6th century CE. Due to the rich silt deposit, this area became an eclectic mix of wetlands, grasslands, saline marshlands, rainforests and mangroves. Naturally, it played host to a rich variety of wildlife – tigers, leopards, elephants, wild buffaloes, rhinoceros, deer and countless species of birds. An even richer variety of flora flourished. Today, despite widespread destruction and the extinction of several species, the Sunderbans' claim to fame is that it is home to the Bengal tiger, besides being a haven to 49 species of mammals, 355 species of birds, over 500 species of plants and 360 species of fish. According to the 2011 tiger census, there are about

270 tigers on the Indian side of the delta. Although previous rough estimates had suggested much higher figures – close to 300 – the 2011 census provided the first-ever scientific estimate of tigers in the area.[2] Equally at home here are estuarine crocodiles, Irrawaddy dolphins, Ganges sharks and innumerable crustaceans and insects.

Recorded human inhabitation of the Sunderbans began somewhere in the 5th century BCE. Historians suggest that the delta was first populated by those who came in from the Gangetic plains in the north – during the reign of Emperor Ashoka and during the Gupta period – and by ships from the southern seas. There were also tribal people who came from the east and west: the Chandals and the Pods, respectively. Forested deltaic lands were first cleared for settlement and then for agriculture. Initially, sustenance depended on fish and fruit from the forest. With the advent of humans came the issues of disease and epidemics. Invasion went hand-in-hand with the shifting of the rivers and their basins and channels, almost until the 12th century CE.

'Just prior to the 5th century BCE the Proto-Australoid (Austic stock) groups, the "Veddoid" or "Kobil", started to settle in the upper parts of the delta. This began a period of sporadic human settlement in the Sunderbans. This organized social and political life in the Bengal basin and such settlements continued all the way to 1100 CE. Forests were periodically cleared for habitation and then abandoned when diseases struck or channels shifted.'[3]

Further invasions continued through the era of the Bengal Sultanate in the 13th and 14th centuries, and in the Mughal era from the 16th–18th centuries. By then, the British had arrived on the scene. In the initial years of the British Raj, Kolkata, then known as Calcutta, was the centre of establishment and the seat of power of the British East India Company – particularly after the Battle of Plassey in 1757 – because of its strategic location. An added benefit was that the impenetrable Sunderbans lay to its south, which to a large extent discouraged foreign invaders.

From the first human habitation of the Sunderbans in the 5th century BCE until the advent of British rule on the Indian subcontinent, the forests of the Sunderbans and the wildlife therein had been greatly damaged. But worse was yet to come. From the mid-1800s onwards, any landowner or zamindar, able to pay the British for it, was allowed to clear forested areas in the delta to own plots of land and to extend existing plots. A few years later, after assuming proprietary rights over it, the British began to lease out land in the Sunderbans to planters for commercial agriculture, especially of paddy. Not only did this cause the forests to fade away, but animals, too, became extinct. A study on this reveals: 'The British soon became dissatisfied with their ventures in the Sunderbans. An appropriate revenue system had not been easily found and so levying revenue on the cultivable lands soon became too cumbersome. On the whole, cultivation in the Sunderbans yielded such mixed results that the British administration abandoned the idea of reclaiming the south-west portions of the Sunderbans for agricultural purposes and concentrated instead on tapping it for fuel resources.'[4]

Despite the degradation of the Sunderbans during the British Raj, there is one Britisher in particular whose presence left a positive mark on the land and its people: Lord Canning, the Governor General of India, and later Viceroy (1856–62), after whom the town of Canning is named. This is the last town one passes through before reaching Godkhali, the gateway to the Sunderbans. Canning, which could also be called an extended gateway to the Sunderbans, is situated along the southern bank of the Matla river. It was here that Lord Canning attempted to establish an alternative port to Kolkata. He had two major reasons: to protect the natural defence structure provided by the forest to the port of Calcutta and therefore, build a township viable for commercial purposes just before the forested area began, and to build a port that rivalled that of Singapore. The town of Canning was built complete with a strand, a marketplace, residential areas and even hotels. Unfortunately, the Viceroy had no control over Mother Nature. During monsoon, the river became turbulent, as it does even today. At low tide, it was (and still is) almost inaccessible. At other times in the year, the river silted up, making it impossible for boats and launches to navigate even close to the port. Only now has commuting in and out of Canning become relatively better, after the construction of a bridge over the Matla river, but at that time it put an end to Lord Canning's plans of establishing a grand port to supplement and support the one at Calcutta. Today, the township is a major supply source of seafood for Kolkata. Fishermen bring the catch of the day to Canning's famous all-night bazaar and the supply is procured by various wholesalers and agents. The town is also a major railway station, connecting different parts of West Bengal to each other through various lines. The closest watchtower in the forest of tides, Sajnekhali, is about five hours away from Canning by boat.

In a land where assorted natural calamities, epidemics and isolated diseases take a toll on human life, a more fearsome killer is on the prowl. While tigers elsewhere are known to kill humans only when they are unable to hunt due to old age or injury, here the Bengal tiger, an animal identified the most with the Sunderbans, has always had a taste for human flesh.

Though there are no definitive views on why this is so, there are a number of theories. 'One theory is that the salinity of the environment somehow gives the tigers the taste for human blood. Another is that the ingestion of so much salt damages a tiger's liver and kidneys, making it irritable. More likely, the tiger has become accustomed to the taste of human flesh as a result of the cyclones and floods, which carry dead bodies down the water channels or strewn about to decompose.'⁵

'Among these islands, it is in many places dangerous to land,' the French explorer François Bernier wrote in 1666, 'for it constantly happens that one person or another falls prey to tigers. These ferocious animals are very apt, it is said, to enter the boat itself, while the people are asleep, and to carry away some victim, who, if we are to believe the boatmen of the country, happens to be the stoutest and fattest of the party.'⁶

Another, possibly far-fetched, theory – and the locals firmly believe in it – is that the tigers here developed a taste for human blood and flesh during the Partition, when India and East Pakistan were created. As millions crossed new borders through the mangroves, some fell prey to the felines, turning them into man-eaters, a tradition that seems to have continued since then.

Also, since the Bengal tiger is a fish-eater and an expert swimmer, it attacks boats laden with fish that are on their way to the marketplaces. The humans occupying the boats come under attack as well. There have been several incidents where boats carrying people even without fish have been attacked.

The ever-growing human population on the delta has had a severe impact on the delicate ecosystem. Reckless destruction during the British era resulted in a near wipe-out of the forests as well as wild animals like leopards and rhinoceroses. Tigers became fewer, not just because of deforestation, but also due to poaching and hunting.

After several pleas, attempts and interventions by wildlife advocates, this was brought under control. A conservation plan was initiated in the early 1900s wherein land leases were banned, reserved areas were marked out and administrative changes were brought about. All this began while the Indian subcontinent was still under the East India Company's jurisdiction. Things truly changed when the subcontinent gained freedom from the British. The Partition caused the Sunderbans to be divided between India and East Pakistan, the latter receiving 60 per cent of the Sunderbans region. The major portion of revenue for this part of Pakistan was from the Sunderbans' forests, which made conservation difficult. When East Pakistan later became Bangladesh, there was a heavy inflow of refugees into India, most of whom were settled in the Indian Sunderbans, thereby clearing out more land for habitation and cultivation. 'On August 18, 1947, the Sunderbans was managed by a single authority – the Sunderbans Division, headquartered at Khulna. Three days later, on August 21, everything changed. Independence from the British created East Pakistan [now Bangladesh] dividing the administration of the Sunderbans with 4,262 sq. km in the 24 Parganas in India in the charge of West Bengal.[7]

The year 1973 was crucial for the Sunderbans, both in India and in Bangladesh. While on the Indian side Project Tiger was launched and the Sunderbans Tiger Reserve was created, on the Bangladeshi side, it was decided to manage the Sunderbans under the Bangladesh Wildlife Preservation Order.

The Sunderbans mangrove forest is now a Ramsar site. The Ramsar Convention, or the Convention of Wetlands, held in the Iranian city of Ramsar, in 1971, is an intergovernmental treaty that provides guidelines for the conservation of wetlands across the globe; it came into force in 1975.[8] From a wildlife sanctuary and a reserved forest, Sunderbans was declared a UNESCO world heritage site in 1987.[9]

Taken as a whole, the Sunderbans is a very remote and hostile area. However, there are divides within the region. Islands closer to the mainland have access to facilities such as means of transportation other than boats and medical infrastructure, making them less at risk from nature's onslaughts. These islands are like little townships compared to others that are located inland and are, therefore, barely accessible. The soil of the former is more arable due to the distance from the rivers that first empty themselves into the sea and then come back salty and ferocious to claim the land at the turn of the tide. The latter, apart from bearing soil unsuitable for cultivation, is also susceptible to tidal waters submerging the entire land in a matter of minutes. On these islands, the embankments built around each village for protection cannot thwart storm and cyclone waters for very long. When the cyclone waters penetrate the embankments and enter the fields, which they often do, arability of the land is lost for long periods.[10] It then takes at least three years for the land to regenerate itself and become suitable for growing crops again. Also, locals living inland are more prone to wildlife attacks due to their proximity to the forest. And in the absence of a medical infrastructure, it is almost impossible to survive a snake bite or crocodile and tiger attacks.

Living in the Sunderbans, there was something to learn every day, which, more often than not, was a lesson in survival in the wilderness. Every evening, I sat outdoors under a canopy of stars and the moon's silvery glow, until I was driven inside by the mosquitoes. The cool breeze from the river helped soothe the unsettling feeling that would have built up during the day: a feeling of uncertainty and insecurity at finding myself all alone on a remote island. Little did I know then that Bali was adopting me as much as I was adopting Bali.

I was bemused by the way everyone in the village got involved in everything, no matter how big or small. New mangrove saplings would be planted by the entire village. The mere act of casting a fishing net in one's brackish water pond for that day's fish would be enough of an event for everyone to gather and comment on the process. How could I possibly stay untouched by this?

The village and its folks were beginning to grow on me like a network of trellises. The main player was Mayna, who took care of my home and my meals. She was an employee of the Foundation from the time of Aila-related relief work. Gregarious and well-connected, Mayna had also been managing the Foundation's affairs in the absence of a permanent representative. She did the banking, organized weekly medical camps, maintained accounts, arranged transportation for volunteers and even identified mangrove saplings for transplantation.

In her early thirties, Mayna had chosen to remain single, an unusual decision which could not have been easy for her to make, considering the obvious familial pressures. She looked after her ailing parents and was the matriarch in a family of 11. Her two brothers were married and had two children each. In this joint family, it was Mayna who decided everything from who needed new clothes to when to sow paddy and vegetable seeds in their fields. She had adopted her elder sister's daughter,

Kuku. Though the child stayed with her parents, it was Mayna who took care of her needs – from paying the school fees to buying the girl gifts on festivals.

Being the only educated member of the family, Mayna commanded the respect of her siblings. Most people in the village looked up to her. She was always consulted – whether it was for buying a new saree or for match-making. She was trained as a barefoot medical worker and made no bones about counselling men and women alike on the need for family planning. As a part of the Foundation, it was Mayna who had made the construction of the volunteers' home possible, a process that was being supervised by another volunteer who was previously based intermittently at Bali. This was a particularly tough task in a land where there were no permanent structures, and where it was prudent to simply bow down to the forces of nature and to acknowledge that there was nothing that could withstand the might of the elements.

The tide changes every six hours, from high to low and vice versa. Twice a day, a fascinating phenomenon takes place in the Sunderbans. As the tide rises, large areas of land, including forested land, get submerged under water. This makes it possible for the boats to ply between the islands. And when the tide recedes, the forests re-emerge as if from hiding. At such times, it is not possible for the boats to navigate too far. The ebb and flow of the tides brings about communication of a different kind between people and animals. During high tide, they are forced to stay within the limits of their respective islands on portions of land that do not get submerged. As the tide changes, both find more space to move about.

Just as humans and animals attained a new equilibrium of co-existence on these islands, different communities of people also learned to get along with equanimity here. Hindus, Muslims and approximately 45 indigenous groups co-exist in relative harmony in different pockets of various villages on each island. The blend of their backgrounds, beliefs, cultures and religious practices has resulted in an eclectic collection of folk tales, legends and myths, and the birth of many deities. Without communal divides, these gods and goddesses are worshipped by everyone, outside the realms of organized religion, and for specific reasons. Manasa Devi, who has a beautiful and magical legend attached to her own birth, parentage and existence, is prayed to for protection against snake bites. Panchu Thakur is the protector of children, while the goddess Devi Tusu bestows fertility upon the land. Dakshin Rai is the god of tigers, Makal Thakur is the god of fish, and Kalu Roy guards people from crocodiles. Chief among the gods is Bon Bibi, who is considered a mother figure by the locals. Everyone prays to her in their time of crisis. Apart from protecting and guiding people, the deities have given rise to a rich diversity of literature – songs, poems, stories and sagas, art and legends.

The story of Bon Bibi begins in the Arabian city of Medina, where her father, a fakir named Berahim, also called Ibrahim, lived. Unable to have children with his first wife, Phulbibi, he married Golalbibi with the assent of Phulbibi, who reserved the right to ask for something in return from him in the future. As the legend goes, with the blessings of Archangel Gabriel, unknown to either the husband or his first wife, Golalbibi conceived. At this point, Phulbibi reminded Berahim of his promise and asked him to leave the pregnant Golalbibi in the forest.

Having given his word, Berahim had no choice but to do what he had promised. All alone in the forest, Golalbibi gave birth to twins – a baby girl, who was named Bon Bibi (the lady of the forest), and her twin brother, Shah Jongoli (the king of the forest). Perhaps daunted by the prospect of raising the children alone in the wilderness, Golalbibi abandoned the babies. They were raised by animals, in particular, a spotted deer. When they came of age, Archangel Gabriel visited them and explained that they had been brought into the world for a specific and special mission: to travel to the country of eighteen tides – the Sunderbans – and make it habitable for human beings. Guided and protected by the universal forces and divine magic, Bon Bibi became the protector of the people who were to inhabit the Sunderbans, while Shah Jongoli protected the forests. Together, they helped alleviate both the remoteness of the wilderness as well as the suffering of the people of the Sunderbans.

During my stay in the Sunderbans, I revisited several times the story of Bon Bibi, the multi-cultural goddess who was called upon by wood-collectors, honey-gatherers and fishermen alike for protection before they entered the forest and exposed themselves to attacks by tigers and other wildlife.

Early in February, a fortnight into my relocation to Bali, I was still familiarizing myself with the little facets of life in the Sunderbans. The work on the structure of the hospital had started. The foundation had been laid, and the walls were being raised. The preparation for the project had begun months before I had arrived in Bali. For Mayna, this had meant getting together a group of people who would fill PET bottles with sand. Most people had smirked and made fun of her when she had initially told them that a massive structure was to be constructed with the bottles. But since this had meant an opportunity to earn money and make a living, some women had come forward and accepted the challenge to be a part of a new concept. Hence, months before the actual work of construction began, sand-filled bottles-cum-bricks were being prepared. The sense of shock I had experienced when I saw mountainous heaps of these ready-and-waiting-to-be-used 'bricks' was something that made me smile every time the memory came back to me. Of course, an unsung part of this whole exercise was gathering bottles all across the city of Kolkata, and having them delivered to Bali, a task entrusted to the Kolkata-based volunteers of the Foundation.

Naturally, the jetty was our lifeline. Goods, especially construction material, were off-loaded here and brought to the hospital's site. Passenger boats would stop by at specific times on fixed days of the week, and the locals would organize their lives around this schedule – purchase of supplies from other islands, visits to the nearby towns, official paperwork, and so on. All these activities required commuting – something that could not be taken for granted.

The existing jetty required constant maintenance. It now also needed reinforcement and an extension in order for it to sustain the immense pulls and pressure, not just from the tide waters but also from the heavy movement of people and goods on it. Given the extent of work required on the jetty, this would involve fresh construction. So not only did we need to organize construction material for the hospital building, but for the jetty as well.

The two days when we were forced to stop work while waiting for fresh construction material to be delivered, presented me with an opportunity to experience living and travelling like a local. Mayna offered to take me on an introductory visit to Gosaba Island. For her, it was a weekly affair to go across the Bidya river to Gosaba, to draw money from the bank to make the weekly payments to the workers. There was a flurry of excitement amongst the workers when they got to know that I was going to make my maiden visit to Gosaba. This meant I was going to travel like a local and it soon became clear to me why everyone was so amused.

When I had made my way to the forest of tides for the first time, I had stepped out of the Kolkata airport, boarded a car and reached the riverfront in the Sunderbans, from which point I was transported by a huge and comfortable cylinder-powered launch to my destination. In Bali, I had disembarked from the boat on to the Foundation's jetty, and walked the 300 metres to reach 'home'. Today, when I stepped out of 'home', I still had to walk 300 metres, but not towards the jetty. There was a dirt track behind the house which led to the market area. Mayna led me down that track to a motorized cycle-van which took us across Bijaynagar through a maze of fields, market squares, tube-well junctions, clusters of huts and even the forest reserve office compound, to a place called

Birajnagar. The entire route being a dirt track, the hour-long journey was exhausting.

The van driver, Prateet-da, was impressed that I wasn't complaining. He teamed up with Mayna to be my local guide. The next part of the journey is one of my most cherished memories of my stay in the Sunderbans. From the ghat at Birajnagar we hopped on to a ferry which took us across the Bidya river. Mayna and I bought the tickets, which, to my amusement, cost only ₹1 each. Other people on the ferry had loaded bicycles and even cattle. The ride lasted a mere five minutes, but it was an experience of a lifetime. As the waves and currents buffeted the boat and it swerved and swung, we lurched from side to side. My heart was in my mouth as I do not know how to swim. At certain points the boat became half submerged and the threat of going under looked imminent. Cries of anguish rose from all of us with each lurch, and almost as if on cue, the cattle moaned, registering deep disapproval of the boatman's stunts.

After disembarking at Gosaba ghat, it took me several minutes to stabilize and start the 10-minute walk to the bank. I realized that it had been almost two hours since we had left home. Even though it was mid-February and the mornings and evenings were chilly, the days were bright, sunny and hot.

The branch of the State Bank of India at Gosaba was the only functional bank in all of the Sunderbans. The sight of the crowd at the bank was as unsettling as the boat journey. Thankfully, our wait in the long queue was short, since we got preferential treatment as the Foundation's account was one of the oldest in the branch. Finishing our work in the bank quickly, we headed off to the local fruit and vegetable market where choice and quality were better than in the Bali market. After the mundane chores of bank work, picking up groceries and other household stuff, Mayna took me around the market, to various shops selling clothes and even silver ornaments. When I checked about bookshops, we were directed to a stationery shop. After picking up a few stationery items, we left all our shopping for safekeeping with this shopkeeper, and headed off to explore the island.

We started with the Hamilton House. Sir Daniel Hamilton (1860–1939) was a Scottish businessman and revolutionary for whom Bengal was a second home. He came to India to oversee the operations of the mercantile firm Mackinnon Mackenzie, first in Bombay and later in Calcutta. He acquired tracts of land on Gosaba, Rangabelia and Satjelia islands, together known as the Gosaba block of islands. In order to improve the living conditions of the locals, he undertook various developmental projects. One of the most important steps was the introduction of the co-operative system, initially in Gosaba and later in the other two islands. An account of Hamilton's activities on the islands says, 'Gosaba island became the headquarters of Hamilton's estate and his three islands were together referred to as "Hamilton-abad", and Hamilton, like a true zamindar, started naming the new villages which sprouted on these islands: Emilybari, Luxbagan, Annpur, Jamespur after family members.'[11] After his retirement, he spent all his time educating and encouraging people to take ownership of and responsibility for their own lives and lands, and established a co-operative society on the lines of the Co-operative Movement which had been initiated in India, especially in the rural hinterlands. His version of the co-operative society dealt with not just agricultural produce, but also matters of credit. He built and started a school, which he preferred to call the rural reconstruction institution. Complete with a marketplace, a dispensary and even roads, the society apparently had no caste divisions, and they even printed their own currency. The island of Gosaba owes its current status to Sir Hamilton and his attempts at creating a Utopian society.

Hamilton built a house for himself on the island, and a smaller one for Rabindranath Tagore. 'The latter even visited the place in December 1932 and with him Hamilton launched the "Gosaba-Bolpur Co-operative Training Institute" whose mission was to train people to launch co-operative societies in India's rural areas.'[12] Both the houses were built on stilts, which is why they have withstood the travails of time and many storms and cyclones. By allowing free passage, the space between the earth and the actual structure neutralizes to a great extent the effect of strong winds and water currents, thereby minimizing damage to the structure.

Mayna and I needed to make our way back to Bali soon if we wanted to get home before sundown. But I was told that, having come so far, we should not leave without visiting the women's co-operative at Rangabelia, the island next to Gosaba, which was connected by road. This meant another van ride, but not as back-breaking as the first one, since we were on tarmac roads. It was a delight to visit the co-operative's store which stocked colourful, hand-printed batik kurtas, bags, bed sheets and even sarees. I needed very little persuasion to shop.

Mayna asked the van driver to use a different route while taking us back to Gosaba. She wanted me to visit what was known as the widows' colony. Seeing my surprise, she told me that each island had a cluster of huts where all the women whose husbands had been killed in wildlife attacks lived together as a community. We visited the house of an old lady, Kokila, who was known to Mayna. During a brief conversation, while we sipped on some hot tea, Kokila-di told us she had been widowed at the age of 23 after seven years of marriage and having borne three children. A tiger had killed her husband when he had gone into the forest along with two other men to collect honey. It had been a life-altering occurrence. While she continued living in the same village, her in-laws suggested she move away from the main house and live in a hut some distance away. They built a new hut for her near where other women who had lost their husbands lived. Her children divided their time between their grandparents and their mother. She was given a small patch of land from her husband's share where she grew her annual supply of paddy and potatoes. She toiled hard for a dignified existence. Remarriage was out of the question, as societal norms did not permit it. Kokila-di had taken the reversals in her stride and was dignity personified. I was told that the widows' colony at Gosaba had better infrastructure than the ones on other islands where the conditions were rather dismal.

After collecting our bags from the stationery shop, we reached the banks of the river. The ferry had been doing brisk business all day. Here, Mayna spotted the *Sundari*, a launch that belonged to the Nature Club, our neighbours, located close to the Foundation's campus on Bali. She made a quick call to Subhash-da, one of the staff members at the Nature Club, to seek permission to hitch a ride. He confirmed that the *Sundari* was on its way back to the Nature Club and told her who was steering the boat. Mayna called the driver of the boat and requested him to take us along. She also did not forget to inform Prateet-da who was supposed to meet us on the other side of the river to take us home on his cycle-van.

After spending an illuminating day at Gosaba, I decided to

spend the second day of my two-day break getting to know my co-workers better.

I was beginning to trust and rely heavily on Jogesh-da and Babu. I visited Jogesh-da's house and realized that his daughter, Molina, was married to Prateet-da. They were expecting their second baby in a few months' time. Molina lived close to the Foundation's campus but she was visiting her parents' house when I went there. I was introduced to Jogesh-da's wife, who worked in the village as a midwife. Molina was relying completely on her mother to see her through the pregnancy. When I advised the two ladies that a proper medical check-up was necessary and important, their response shut me up. A bumpy ride on the van and a treacherous crossing of the river to get to the one and only government hospital in Gosaba for a regular check-up every few weeks... Wasn't that a bigger risk for the unborn child and the mother?

Babu was the son of the Foundation's night guard, Guru-da, who had received me at the jetty on the night of my arrival in the Sunderbans. Babu took on responsibilities without being asked to do so. He needed no prodding and was always around to help with chores – fixing a leak in the water tank, lifting furniture in the house, a quick visit to the shops to buy provisions… Later on, when the construction picked up speed, Subroto, Babu's brother, also became an indispensable part of the work team. The two brothers could lift heavy weights and either could single-handedly do jobs that otherwise required three men. I knew I could fall back upon these families in my hour of need, no matter how dire it was. I felt blessed to have such support.

At the Foundation's jetty in Bijaynagar, as at Godkhali, the loading and off-loading of material was dependent not just on the tides, but also on the whims of the labour union. During the previous years, there had been some misunderstanding, and therefore, unpleasantness, between the coolies and the Foundation. As a result, they resisted my requests to speed up work. Sometimes, the boat with the material had to wait for hours on end before the *muthias* arrived on the scene. At other times, they refused to do the work, which meant that I had to get the workers working on both the construction sites – the hospital building and the jetty – to stop work and off-load the boat. After repeated occurrences of such situations, I decided it was time to settle the matter permanently.

One morning, the boat arrived at 5 a.m. I called up Shakti-da, the head of the *muthia* union in Bijaynagar, and informed him of the boat's arrival. He already knew about it as it was the supplier's job to tie up with the union and exchange information on the various boats that were to arrive at the several jetties on the island during the week. The union accordingly divided their time among these boats. Shakti-da told me that he and his team were likely to arrive an hour later, which they did. They found me waiting for them at the jetty with packets of biscuits and hot tea, prepared by the omnipresent Mayna, whom I had told that I intended to sort out the issues with the *muthias*. She had offered to come along, but I felt it was best to do this on my own.

When I invited the *muthias* to have tea and biscuits, they said they had a lot of work for the day and declined my offer. Reluctant to let this opportunity go, I told them that work could wait and that it was necessary to sort out pending issues cordially. When I apologized for any misunderstandings in the past, they seemed to relent. While we were sipping tea, I explained to them the importance of building the jetty and the hospital. Two of them, Narayan and Horen, showed more understanding than the others and agreed that the hospital would be quite beneficial. They recounted how older people, expectant mothers and, in particular, critical patients lost their lives because they were unable to reach Gosaba in time. Apparently, more than half the new-borns in the Sunderbans did not survive beyond two days due lack of pre- and post-natal medical facilities. Realizing my struggle with my inadequate Bangla, they switched to their broken Hindi. They addressed me as *Didi*. Though still an outsider, it seemed as if I was accepted by them. From that day, the Foundation's work was always given priority. As word reached the Godkhali union about this meeting, we noticed a change of attitude in them, too.

Just as I thought everything was falling into place, the Foundation was served a notice by the panchayat. We were asked to stop work and present ourselves at the panchayat ghar in a locality called Kalitola. Apparently, when the Foundation's jetty was being constructed, before I had arrived in Bali to start work on the hospital project, four mangrove saplings had been destroyed. It was a punishable offence according to the laws of the Forest Department, and we were under scrutiny for having committed a crime. Mayna and I walked the 10-minute distance from the Foundation's campus to reach the panchayat ghar and found ourselves in a room full of at least 40 men who, the moment they laid their eyes on us, started a chorus of myriad accusations. Many villagers were present wanting to watch the happenings. Overwhelming as it was, the situation demanded a quick and firm response.

In my limited Bangla, I requested that I be given a chance to speak. I apologized for the unwitting crime we had committed. Then I promised that the Foundation would plant 1,000 mangrove saplings along the village embankment. I told them that while four saplings may have been destroyed, this only happened because we were trying to provide a hospital for the healthcare and well-being of the locals. The construction and stabilization of the new jetty was a precursor for the hospital to which people from all surrounding islands could also come for treatment. Could they not forgive the Foundation in the interests of the betterment of their own people? A debate ensued where some of the panchayat members argued that if we were allowed to go scot-free, it would set a precedent and others would not think twice before destroying mangroves. Some others said that as the mangroves were destroyed for a purpose, it was justified. At this point, the meeting turned noisy and chaotic. After consulting amongst themselves, the office-bearers eventually allowed Mayna and I to leave, though not before being officiously reprimanding and warning us not to repeat the crime.

It later came to light that there were local politics and bruised egos at play. While the damage to the mangrove saplings was the only ostensible reason to pull me up, there were other reasons for which I was summoned. In fact, there was a litany of misdemeanours – I had chosen to live alone and walk around unchaperoned; I had refused to hire some youngsters from the village for the construction work (I had not hired them because they had shown little interest in the work); and, most importantly, I had gone about doing my job, paying no heed to the protocol in terms of taking the permission of the village elders before commencing the work. While some of the people found this insulting, many villagers were openly positive about the Foundation and its work and chose to support us. It appeared that we were becoming a force to reckon with in Bijaynagar, and this, I gathered, had ruffled a few feathers.

In Bijaynagar, the day began at dawn, since the inhabitants of this magical land did not want to lose even a single minute of daylight. As the sun set, it took along with it the hustle and bustle of the day, forcing the villagers to retire to their homes for want of anything else to do. Another reason why everything went quiet after dusk was that the surrounding forest of mangroves was inhabited by tigers. There had been many instances of tiger sightings, and more for the sake of their own life and limb than any respect for the big cat, the villagers chose to remain indoors. The villagers believed it was inauspicious even to say the word *bagh* (tiger) and that the very sound of the word would attract the animal to them.

All the houses in the village, built by the same method, looked similar: mud structures with one or two partitions dividing the interior into utility rooms. A part of the earth was dug up and the soil was used to create a raised platform on which the huts were constructed. The elevation was done with the fond hope that the water levels, when they did rise in the case of a cyclone or storm, would not go higher than the platform. The kitchen was almost always outdoors – a small, temporary structure constructed either out of mud or palm leaves, or both. The dwellings of the poor and the relatively affluent had only one difference. Those who could afford it used tin sheets for their roofs, which were then covered with thatch. The windows of these houses mostly had steel grills, and were not mere holes in the wall. Every household reared hens, ducks, goats and cows – their numbers a proof of the relative affluence of the family. The eggs, milk and meat were primarily for the family's consumption; what could be spared was sold.

The area from where the soil was dug up to make the platform was left open, and turned into a fresh water pond when rainwater filled it up. This water was used for bathing, washing clothes and utensils, and other household needs. People also bred fish and prawns in some ponds. While the crops were growing, this water was used for irrigation. For drinking water, the women would usually queue up at tube wells. Potable, non-saline water was also ferried in jerrycans from Godkhali and sold at many of the islands. I had heard stories of women swimming across the river and back, while balancing a pot of drinking water from a tube well on their heads. The fact that there could be a paucity of clean water in a land that had eighteen rivers flowing through it was bewildering for me.

The centre of the village had a clutch of shops which looked as if they were huddling together. There was a carpenter's shop, a tailor's shop, and a dark, shabby tea shop. That made up the whole market. For anything more than select vegetables, soap, eggs and, of course, *bidis*, one had to cross the river and go to Gosaba. The tea shop acted as a meeting point for the young and the old alike, since it had a solar-battery-operated television.

Another well-frequented spot was the faucet of tube well, by the side of a solar-powered street light. While there was almost an unending procession of women from early morning to fill their pitchers, the tube well was visited by men, women and children through the day, either for a bath in the public or simply for a drink of water. In the evenings, the solar battery-operated street light was a big draw. Men of all age groups gathered under it. It was a public forum in every sense. Upcoming weddings, decisions which had a bearing on the general welfare of the village, the latest news from the Forest Department and the feasibility of growing a second crop of paddy – all were topics of discussion here.

One of the stark features of the Sunderbans is the abject poverty of the locals due to the absence of livelihood opportunities. Often, men go missing for a few days. They venture deep into the forest, sometimes illegally, into the reserved areas meant strictly for wildlife, where the cutting of trees is prohibited. Most men return after gathering wood and honey, perhaps some fish and crabs, and even prawn seed from the rivers. A small fraction of this is consumed by the household and the major portion is sold in nearby markets for value equivalent to only a few meals. But this is fraught with a big risk. A wild animal attack is always imminent in the forest.

According to Mayna, while going deep into the jungle, men wear masks with human facial features on the back of their heads in the belief that a wild animal attacks from behind and wearing a mask on the back of the head might confuse the animal, thereby preventing such an attack. A small prayer ceremony is always held in honour of Bon Bibi, the guardian spirit of the forest, before the men venture into the forest.

The women, meanwhile, observed a strange custom. Whenever their men went into the forest, they abandoned their coloured sarees and dressed in the white garb of a widow. Bangles and sindoor, the traditional markers of being married, were eschewed and they moved around with a funereal look. Early widowhood is common in the Sunderbans and it seems that by pretending to be a widow, the women hoped to turn this around, or at least trick fate and prevent it from happening for as long as possible.

Since its intervention in the Sunderbans post Aila, the Foundation had introduced a weekly charitable medical camp on the island. Held each Thursday at the volunteers' home on the Foundation's campus, the camp was also attended by patients from nearby islands. Two doctors would come from Kolkata and examine nearly 500 patients. People from within the island – from places as far away as Amla Methi and Pocket Nine, nearly an hour's ride on a cycle-van – would begin queuing up as early as 2 a.m. I discovered this when, one night, I was woken up by several voices speaking at once. Turning on the bedside lamp, feeling grateful that it had worked – which meant that the solar-powered battery had lasted – I checked the time on my phone: it was 2:45 a.m. Accustomed as I was to the city's conveniences and availability of doctors almost on call, it took me quite a while to accept that, in this land, visiting a doctor was a whole-day affair.

On that day, like any other day of the camp, the patients first queued up before the break of dawn, and then waited for the gates to open up at 8 a.m. so that they could have their names registered for a check-up. People then dispersed to sit and wait under the shade of the *keora* or other trees growing in the courtyard. This went on until the doctors arrived by late morning, considering it was a journey of approximately four to five hours to reach Bali from Kolkata.

Once the doctors arrived, a buzz went through the compound. The doctors wasted no time and got down to work almost immediately. The patients began to queue up again, anxiety written all over their faces and body language.

I watched through a blur of emotions how old people, almost bent over, with contorted bodies and their various ailments, listened with reverence to every word uttered by the doctor. When asked to do medical tests, most patients told the doctors that neither did they know where to go for the tests nor could they afford them. There was a sense of disappointment in their voices, perhaps at the failure of the state and governmental agencies to look after their basic needs. An unexplainable heaviness took over my usually carefree disposition.

After completion of the physical examinations, the patients queued up again to receive the prescribed medicines. This was managed by Mayna, who was assisted by some dedicated youths from the village. Even in late February the day was hot and humid, and it was getting worse as the hours progressed. The queue of anxious people was not even half done when it was time to break for lunch. My dampened spirits could barely keep up a polite conversation with the doctors during the meal.

Getting back to work right after lunch, the doctors showed no signs of the distress and melancholy that I was going through. Perhaps they were inured to such situations, or perhaps, they were trained not to display emotions. I gathered some courage and struck up conversations with some of the waiting patients. There was little other than abject poverty in the lives of the local people. A majority of them could barely afford two meals a day. With hardly enough food to eat, nutrition was not something they were concerned about.

It was evening by the time all the patients had been seen by the doctors and given medicines. After a hard day's work, the doctors could not resist the tea Mayna had prepared. The sun was about to set, and though this was usually my favourite time of the day, today my spirits were low. I decided to spend some time sitting quietly by the river. As I rewound and replayed the day in my mind, I realized that there were no employment opportunities in the village whatsoever. Except for growing some rice and vegetables, mostly for self consumption, there wasn't much a person could do in the Sunderbans. Whatever little was surplus was sold at the local *haat* every Wednesday. With no pukka housing, public buildings, water supply network, sewage and sanitation, there was no demand for electricians and plumbers. There were a few masons and carpenters around, though. Other than these, all the men in the village worked as daily-wage labourers if there was construction of some kind taking place. But how many buildings did one village need anyway?

Meanwhile, the walls of the hospital were coming along fine. The twin entrances to the building were designed to prevent flooding of the hospital in the eventuality of a cyclone. Both entrances were built on a platform five feet high. So, to enter the hospital building, one needed to first climb up a flight of stairs, and then climb down the same height.

In early February, on Saraswati Puja, I received an invitation from the senior secondary school, Vidya Mandir, to visit its campus and be a part of the celebrations. Other than the school in Gosaba, this was the only senior secondary school in the vicinity. About 300 children from nearby islands were day-scholars here and the school provided boarding facility for approximately 100 boys and girls from faraway islands. While most teachers at the school were residents of Bali, there were some teachers who were posted here from outside the Sunderbans. This was an appropriate opportunity to present myself to the community and attempt to get their acceptance.

There were some village elders who were still suspicious of my presence and participating in the local festivities, I was sure, would help my cause.

Mayna and I set out with Prateet-da, on his cycle-van, to visit the school. The welcome extended to us by the principal, Sukumar-da, was overwhelming. Eventually, he became my local guardian and mentor and we established a strong friendship. We participated in the puja along with the students and teachers of the school, who were dressed in their colourful best, with most female teachers and students choosing to wear traditional red-and-white Bengali *taant* sarees. The air was festive, with Rabindra-*sangeet* playing loudly on the campus and colours, flowers and sounds of cheer and laughter in the air. We were treated to a sumptuous lunch thereafter, served in the traditional way, on banana leaves.

There was a fair with small kiosks selling vegetables from the villagers' kitchen gardens. It was the end of the winter season, and some greens were still available, in addition to cauliflower, pumpkins and bitter gourd. There were, of course, shops selling the catch of the day: varieties of fish, prawns and crabs. The most colourful part of the fair was the corner selling sarees and bangles.

The Vidya Mandir campus, that day, was an outstanding example of communal harmony. Hindus and Muslims prayed alongside each other to Saraswati, the Hindu goddess of knowledge and wisdom. Most of them lived in the same neighbourhood in absolute harmony. They bought gifts for each other and ate together. There was occasional strife between the two communities but it was not due to religious differences. These instances of small victories and unity helped buoy my spirit amidst daunting tasks, in a land famous for its fickle temper towards humans.

Despite the warmth I was received with, I quickly learnt that I would have to be discerning in my dealings with the locals. When I had just started working in the Sunderbans, there was a suggestion that we strengthen the Foundation's jetty by spreading 'porcupine shells' in its vicinity, in an attempt to stabilize it. The 'shells' were believed to absorb the pull and push of *jwaar* and *bhaata*, and reduce their direct impact on the jetty. The shells were made by slicing bamboo vertically, and nailing several such slats together to create a zig-zag structure. A fishnet was strung over the middle of this structure to hold in clay bricks. Once these porcupine shells are submerged in the waters around the jetty, the bricks act as the anchor and prevent them from floating away. Minimizing the force of the water, these structures make the jetty less vulnerable to the tides.

The work for laying the porcupine shells was given to a contractor recommended by the village elders. He started the work – for which he was charging a hefty amount – with many promises and reassurances. After half the shells were made, we decided to drop them in the waters while the other half were still being made, so that the structure of the jetty would already have some protection from the tides. After this was done, the contractor stopped the work, claiming he needed to go away for a pressing family matter. He promised to return after a few days.

Even before the contractor could return, there were reports from at least three places from across the island that the porcupine shells were floating away from near our jetty and landing up at different places. It began to dawn upon us that we had been cheated. The contractor had not put enough number of bricks in each shell, and the currents were taking away the underweighted shells. Of course, he never came back to finish his work. Even though he had not been paid the full amount of the contract, he had still made enough money by short-changing us on the bricks. The village elders, on whose recommendation the contractor had been chosen, casually consoled us by saying that one couldn't trust anybody these days!

The need of the hour was to repair the existing jetty and to extend it. Keeping aside what had already happened, we needed to move ahead.

# Water

—

## Mythology of the Land of Eighteen Tides

In the beginning of time, Brahma the Creator reverentially washed the feet of Vishnu the Preserver, and collected that sacred water in his *kamandal* (stoup). The personification of this holy water, a maiden called Ganga, was brought up in heaven. A childless king named Sagara pleased the gods with his penance and was granted a boon of 60,000 sons. Kapila Muni, a sage and incarnation of Lord Vishnu, lived in his ashram on Sagara Island, named after the ruler. When the king decided to perform the Ashwamedha *yagya*, a jealous Lord Indra stole the sacrificial horse during the ceremonial observances, and hid it near Kapila Muni's ashram.

King Sagara sent his sons to look for the horse. They found it tethered in the Muni's ashram. The Muni, who was deep in meditation, was rudely woken up from it by the shouts of the princes accusing him of stealing the horse. The infuriated Muni, who was opening his eyes after many years of meditation, cast a wrathful glance and reduced the 60,000 princes to ashes.

The matter was investigated by a cousin, Bhagirath, and the misunderstanding and confusion was finally revealed. He begged Kapila Muni to save the souls from eternal damnation, as their last rites had not been performed. The sage agreed but said that could happen only if the maiden Ganga came down to earth and agreed to wash away the sins of the sons herself. Bhagirath then pleaded with Lord Brahma to request Ganga to descend to earth. The maiden felt insulted at being asked to perform such a degrading chore. To take revenge, she decided to descend on earth all at once, flooding the land with her fury. Bhagirath solicited Lord Shiva's help to contain the waters. The Lord agreed because he knew the earth would not be able to withstand the impact of the falling water. When Ganga came to know of this, she decided to alarm Shiva and descended on his head. But the blue god peacefully trapped her in his hair, and released her in streams all over the earth. When the waters washed over Sagara Island, the souls of the 60,000 sons were cleansed, as the sacred waters washed away their ashes.

Sagara Island, or Sagardweep, the spot where the waters of the Ganga touched the earth first, is considered to be the mouth of the Sunderbans. Makar Sankranti, the harvest festival, also a day marked for revering the Sun god, Surya, which falls in mid-January, is regarded as the day on which the Ganga descended to the earth.

An annual Gangasagar Mela (fair) and pilgrimage is held at Sagara Island's southern tip, where the Ganga enters the Bay of Bengal. Thousands of Hindu pilgrims visit the temple constructed here in honour of sage Kapil Muni. The original temple, built two centuries ago, went under water as a result of a natural phenomenon, during British reign. Subsequently, a new temple was built, which is now facing the same threat due to rising sea levels.

Today, not just the temple, but Sagardweep itself is losing the battle for survival due to coastal erosion, unusual tidal activity and cyclones. The island is gradually disappearing into the sea. Like most other islands in the Sunderbans, Sagardweep is also marked by a dry, brown landscape dotted with huts and fields. The infrastructure is better than most other islands because of the influx of tourists for the annual Gangasagar fair.

Apart from regular pilgrims, Sagardweep is also visited by Naga sadhus on the day of the Gangasagar Mela. These sadhus are a particular group of Shaivite saints who reside in caves in the Himalayas and come down to the plains only during festivals like the Kumbh Mela and the Gangasagar Mela.

I visited the fair out of curiosity and to experience local culture. Other than the usual stalls of food, clothes, souvenirs, etc., I also discovered a cock-fight arena. Organized purely for purposes of entertainment, the pomp and show around the arena added to the festive air. The shouts and screams emanating from the fighting pit drew a large number of people. Two large roosters, bred and reared for cock-fighting, were released by their owners. The birds' legs were fitted with tiny knives or spikes. As soon as the birds saw each other, they immediately rushed to attack. The crowd of people gathered around to witness the fight cheered them on by their names: Heera and Sonu. The fight lasted for about five minutes and ended when Heera delivered a lethal blow to Sonu. Several hands exchanged money, as the crowds had engaged in heavy betting. While the triumphant owner of Heera took the bird away to treat it to goodies, Sonu was taken away presumably to be sold as meat.

As March arrived, I realized I had been living and working in the Sunderbans for close to two months. The work on the hospital building was picking up speed, but our brave jetty was slowly buckling under the heavy loads passing over it and the tide waters pulling and pushing at its legs. It was showing signs of disintegration. It was imperative to keep our only connection to the world outside safe. I requested Jogesh-da and our head mason, Panchu-da, to help me review the jetty's structure.

The situation was grim. Immediate action was needed. There was a tone of reprimand in the voices of the villagers when speaking on this matter. An old man told us that when the jetty's construction was being planned, the villagers had advised the Foundation's representatives to consult the village priest for an auspicious date, conduct a ceremonial puja, and only then commence the work. Today, as the person on the ground, I was at the receiving end of their accusations, and was being chastised for ignoring sound advice.

We sent word to the various masons in the village – other than the ones already working on the hospital – that the Foundation would be looking out to give a contract for the repair work of the jetty.

A big crowd gathered at the jetty the following morning. A few masons – those who were willing to work with someone who had no formal training in construction, who had only recently learnt to distinguish cement from sand and mud, who worked irrespective of weather conditions and all other circumstances, who cared very little for protocol as far as panchayat and official matters were concerned – did turn up.

Then there was Bapi-da, who said Lord Vishwakarma and Ma Bon Bibi had visited him in his dream the night before and had told him to work on fixing the jetty with no inhibitions whatsoever. They had assured him that the jetty would

53

withstand all disruptive forces! Accepting this as a sign from the powers that be, I gave the contract for the repair work of the jetty to him.

It was almost the end of May, and the monsoon was just around the corner. While there was a general sense of relief – reprieve from water shortage, the heat and humidity – the overtones of caution in the words of the locals were palpable when they spoke of the impending rains. Commuting between islands would now become more dangerous and difficult. Sources of livelihood would be affected, since access to the forest would be limited in the turbulent waters. Since the soil was clayey, moving around the village, too, would be hazardous in the rains, as people were bound to slip and hurt themselves. Motorized vans would get stuck in the slush. Daily life in the islands would come to a standstill when the rains came down in torrents for days together.

It had been nearly five months since my arrival here and along with the change in seasons, I was witnessing another change. The initial apprehension of the villagers of working with the Foundation had now given way to pride at being part of the team that worked on the construction site. The people of Bali had realized that the hospital was not something for the benefit of the Foundation. It was for them: the people of the Sunderbans. More workers were ready to sign up. This meant that lifting heavy pillars and so on were no longer daunting; it was just the opposite. There was a chirpiness in the workers and they would suddenly break into a song. Choruses like these became common:

*Hai-re-hai . . . hai-yah*

*Jibon jaaye . . . hai-yah*

*Jibon-e-dhani . . . hai-yah*

*Chand badauni . . . hai-yah*

*Badan-e-jama . . . hai-yah . . .*

(While the words of this song meant that life was not easy, in this particular situation, it was making it easier for the workers to lift the heavy weights.)

Myths and legends still hold a lot of power in the Sunderbans. This is the land of eighteen tides: *athhero bhatir desh*. Sitting on the banks of the Bidya river, I was engrossed in watching the hermit crabs that had taken shelter in the abandoned shells left behind by sea snails. These crustaceans do not have a very hard shell, so they use old, discarded shells for their protection. As the hermit crabs grow in size, they need to look out for, and move into, bigger shells.

The numerous brackish water ponds created by the tides near the jetty were a world of their own: water lilies and lotuses bloomed alongside; frogs and fish co-habited; wild grass and fragile-looking underwater plants existed in complete harmony next to each other. Just around the ponds, mud banks that looked like melting chocolate held another parallel world. Cleverly camouflaged in this slush would be mudskippers, crabs, snakes and at times even monitor lizards and crocodiles. They would emerge as and when they pleased, nurturing the fragile ecosystem with their daily survival habits.

The fragrance of the flowering *sirish* tree created the illusion of a pine forest, as the weather had recently changed from hot and dry to hot and humid, announcing the approaching monsoon. Walking through the village, along the dam which ran through the market area, was equally delightful. At many places, the previous day's tides would have brought and deposited hermit crabs in their borrowed shells.

The myriad shades and antics of some of the rivers that I cruised through during my stay in the Sunderbans were fascinating. The eighteen rivers of the Indian side of the Sunderbans are: Ganga, Brahmaputra, Meghna, Padma, Bidyadhari, Gumdi, Hooghly, Pirkhali, Kalindi, Harinbhanga, Matla, Herobhanga, Raimangal, Gosaba, Ichhamati, Thakuran, Nethi and Durga-Dhwani. All of the rivers evoke awe, respect and reverence from the locals. Not surprising, considering that at times, the rise and drop in the water levels, with the changing tides, can be as drastic as 15–20 feet.

These rivers have marked out their trajectory, the nature and path of which has kept changing not just with time but also with the tides. The essence of the Sunderbans lies in these water bodies – the channels, creeks and canals formed by the various rivers – that make every part of the region accessible by boats, and supported by mudflats and mangroves. Each river also has its own story and history. The Matla is the coming together of three rivers: Bidyadhari, Khuratya and Rampura Khaljoin, near Canning town, from where they flow together to meet with the Bay of Bengal. The Bidyadhari, in turn, is a branch of the Hooghly, which has seen majestic days in its royal past when it was navigable. Sadly, it's now an outlet for sewage and excessive rain water from Kolkata. Ichhamati, which means being able to take whatever shape and form one desires, is a source of fresh water supply to the rivers Gosaba and Raimangal. The river Gosaba is born after the numerous canals of the Matla and Raimangal rivers join hands.

The river Nethi has an enchanting legend associated with it. It is linked with the life story of a powerful goddess of the Sunderbans: Manasa Devi. The local legend of her birth is different from the more prevalent Hindu myths. According to the local variation of the myth, when the king of snakes,

Vasuki, was sculpting an idol in the likeness of his mother, Lord Shiva, who was passing by, was inflamed by the idol's beauty. Just then, Chandi, his wife, called out to him and he had to hide his erection. He ejaculated and the divine semen fell on the idol, impregnating it. Thus was born Manasa. She was named so because her birth was the result of sex that had taken place in Shiva's mind.

A mortified Shiva tried to hide this episode by leaving the baby girl in a snake pit where thousands of snakes were hatching. The baby snakes protected Manasa from the cold and the heat, embracing her with their tails. But the fluids from the sharp scales that protected their tender underbellies seared her skin and made it slimy. She also turned a bluish-black colour, as though she had swallowed venom.

The snakes carried Manasa out of the snake pit and bathed her in the Adi Ganga. They fed her and became her cradle and her swing. Black, white and red snakes became her ornaments; their tails became her garments. When she came of age, Vasuki took Manasa to her father, Shiva, who tried to marry her. When she opened her third eye to curse him, he realized who she was. Her dazzling beauty made Chandi jealous. She began to conspire to drive her away, while Manasa tried hard to win the love of her father and step-mother.

During the churning of the Ocean of Milk, it was Manasa who saved Shiva from the deadly venom he swallowed. But

Chandi was so envious that she stabbed her in the eye when she was asleep. Later, when Chandi kicked her to the ground, Manasa, with a single intense look from her third eye, turned Chandi into a statue. Shiva begged her to revive Chandi, which she did. But soon after, he abandoned Manasa again under the shade of a tree, ordering her to never set foot in her father's home. When her tears of anger and hatred fell on the ground, Netra was born. Entrusting the job of looking after Manasa to Netra, Shiva vanished from the scene. Manasa, who had been gentle and loving, became a fury, always quarrelsome and vengeful. In many versions of the myth, Manasa is depicted as being quite dependent on Netra, her advisor, traditionally portrayed as a washerwoman, for ideas and moral support.

To get rid of Manasa, Shiva then fixed her marriage with the sage Jagatkaru. Snakes became her bridal clothes and ornaments. Chandi played her mischief again and let some frogs into the bridal chamber. The snakes that bedecked Manasa got distracted and chased the frogs, thus leaving Manasa naked and furious. Jagatkaru ran away in horror and disbelief. Shiva had to threaten him to return to his daughter. To quickly absolve himself of his duties, Jagatkaru produced a son with Manasa, Astika, and fled. Once again, she was abandoned. Manasa refused to forgive those who did not respect her. She had to always suffer insult, betrayal and orphanhood. Only the tribals who lived in the delta were willing to accept the black, orphaned goddess. Thus, the unrecognized daughter of the God of Destruction remained beyond the pale of Hindu faith, as the untouchable goddess of the dark-skinned and the poor, always craving to be accepted. Over time, however, she was given a place amongst the gods and goddesses worshipped by the so-called higher castes. However, the delta seems to be an apposite place for her – ignored by mainland India and the rest of the world – for it is here that Manasa has found her true believers and is loved and revered.

According to the more prevalent myths of her birth, Manasa is said to be the daughter of sage Kashyapa and Kadru, the mother of snakes. Manasa was identified as the goddess of fertility and marriage rites and was assimilated into the Shaiva pantheon as a relative of Shiva. Myths glorified her by describing in great detail how she saved Shiva after he drank poison, and venerated her as the 'remover of poison'. As a consequence, stories attributing Manasa's birth to Shiva emerged and, ultimately, Shaivism adopted this indigenous goddess into the tradition of mainstream Hinduism. As with most Hindu gods and demi-gods, there are multiple tales associated with Manasa, all with a large numbers of believers. In fact, in the Sunderbans, there is a local parallel to the fable of Manasa's acceptance as goddess.

An influential merchant, Chand Sadagar, who had built a massive city spread across the Sunderbans, was a faithful devotee of Shiva. He had eight sons and the origin of the primitive tribe Chandra-bandhe is attributed to him. As a staunch worshipper of Shiva, he said that the hand that worships Shiva will never worship another god or goddess. And since Chand Sadagar did not worship Manasa, nobody in the entire city worshipped her. Manasa was furious at this. She destroyed seven of his eight sons, yet Chand Sadagar did not relent.

The eighth son, Lokhinder, was to marry a woman named Behula. Manasa decided to kill him on his wedding night. She tried to persuade Vishwakarma, who was a mason, and was given the task of building a house for the couple-to-be, to help her out. Initially, he refused, but when Manasa enticed him with a boon that the people would worship him in the same way that they would eventually worship her, he couldn't resist. He agreed that in the house he had to build for Lokhinder and Behula, he would leave a small hole through which Manasa could enter as a snake and kill Lokhinder. The plan went through and Lokhinder was killed.

Behula refused to cremate the body of her husband. She asked her father-in-law to build her a raft with wood and banana leaves. She wanted to be set afloat with her husband's body, in quest for something or someone who would bring her dead husband back to life. Chand Sadagar heeded Behula's request.

Floating down a river, Behula, with her dead husband's head resting on her lap, saw a washerwoman busy washing clothes. The washerwoman had, earlier, apparently annoyed by her son's mischief, beaten him unconscious. Behula was horrified to learn of this. She splashed some water on the face of the unconscious lad, who came around. Nethi, the washerwoman, brushed Behula aside, saying she didn't have time to waste since she had to finish washing the clothes of the gods who had employed her. Behula requested to be given a chance to do the same. The washerwoman let her do it, in consideration of Behula reviving her son.

When the clothes were washed, the washerwoman took Behula along with her to Devnagari, the land of the gods, to deliver the washed clothes. Impressed and happy with the job well done, the gods said Behula could ask for a boon. She requested that her husband be brought back to life. The gods decided to first find out the reason for his death. When they discovered Manasa was responsible, aware that only she could bring Lokhinder back to life, they summoned her. Manasa was adamant that she would revive Lokhinder only if Chand Sadagar would worship her. Behula was equally adamant that if she were a virtuous and righteous woman, her husband should be brought back to life without any pre-conditions.

Realizing the impasse, the gods requested Shiva to intervene.

Whether this was done because it was an open secret that Manasa was Shiva's daughter is ambiguous and debatable. Nevertheless, because of Shiva's intervention, an agreement was reached upon. Chand Sadagar would worship Manasa, but with his left hand. Also, the offerings made to her would be thrown back over the shoulder, and not in the manner in which offerings are reverentially placed in front of the Shiva *linga*. To agree to this, Manasa placed a further condition that Vishwakarma, too, should be worshipped as a god. She had to honour the promise made to Vishwakarma for his help. Chand Sadagar agreed and Manasa revived Lokhinder. Seeing Chand Sadagar worship Manasa and Vishwakarma, the people of the Sunderbans also followed suit. Thus, Manasa found the acceptance and reverence that she had sought. Initially hailed as the deity of the untouchables and the tribals, worshipped only by the 'lower' castes, she was later included in the pantheon of gods worshipped by 'higher' caste Hindus. She is now regarded as a Hindu goddess rather than a tribal one. The washerwoman, Nethi, could be the Netra of Hindu mythology. And the spot where Behula met her is called Nethidhopani, the word *dhopani* meaning 'to wash'. As a mark of his gratitude to the gods for bringing his son back to life, a temple was built there by Chand Sadagar. Ruins of a temple and a city have been found in the Baghmara forest block of the Sunderbans, thus giving some credence to the legend. It is said that the city built by Chand Sadagar later fell into the hands of Portuguese pirates, salt smugglers and dacoits in the 17th century.

The various myths of Sunderbans, which overlap and keep evolving, depending on who you hear them from, lend credence to the fact that the delta has been inhabited since ancient times. According to early historians and Greek travellers, the ancient name of the Sunderbans was Ganga Rashtra, Ganga's kingdom. This is mentioned in Greek historian and explorer Megasthenes' book *Indica*, now lost, but partially reconstructed from the writings of later authors. The capital of Ganga Rashtra was Gangey Rejia, situated on the east side of river Bhagirathi, which was a famous port once, and located on present-day Sagara Island.

Excavations have also found remains of a Buddhist temple, dated 1668 CE, at the banks of the river Mani. Stone idols dedicated to Surya, the Sun god, indicate the presence of the Maurya dynasty, while excavated currency, a royal seal, and a temple at Mandir Tola at Sagara Island are proof of the presence of the Gupta dynasty.

The Portuguese first came and settled at Tarda Port on the banks of river Bidya in 1590 CE. Regular theft and robberies, and oppression of the locals were common occurrence. Soon, the Sunderbans began to be known as *Moger Muluk*, 'land of thugs'. Under the instructions of Mughal Emperor Aurangzeb, Portuguese pirates were chased away by Mughal prince Suja, and Mir Jumla, the commander-in-chief. The pirates took shelter at Sagara Island, building a fort for themselves. But a heavy flood in 1688 CE caused widespread destruction of the Sunderbans and the fort was destroyed. In 1737 CE, the entire population of the Sunderbans was annihilated due to cyclones, extreme flooding and a subsequent earthquake.

The recent history of human settlement in the Sunderbans dates from the treaty of 1757 signed by Mir Jafar, under which the lands of the district of 24 Parganas were ceded to the East India Company.[1] Mir Jafar betrayed Siraj-ud-Daulah at the Battle of Plassey and subsequently, these lands became the *jagir* or property of Lord Clive. He was the first Nawab of Bengal with the support of the British East India Company. His rule is widely considered as the beginning of British imperialism in India and was a key step in the eventual British domination of vast areas of the subcontinent.[2] In the year 1770, Collector General Claud Russel leased out the land of the Sunderbans for cultivation. Five years later, Major William Tali started indigo plantations there. By 1784, Governor-General Lord Warren Hastings had allowed the jungles of the Sunderbans to be leased to zamindars. This was the beginning of a continuous reclamation of forest land for agriculture.

Widespread deforestation led the British to finally take notice of the depletion of natural resources. They put into action a conservation plan. In 1817, the first departmental head of the Sunderbans was appointed by the British government, a deputy forest officer named Sir M.U. Green and the first commissioner was William Dampier. Dividing the Sunderbans into blocks in 1828, the East India Company officially declared the forests and its resources as their property. In 1830, Commissioner Dampier and Survey Officer Hedges drew a straight line to mark the northern boundary of the active delta, which came to be known as the Dampier–Hedges line.

In 1851, the first Electric Telegraph Department of India was established at Diamond Harbour. A subsequent railway line was established – Champahati Railway Service – to import and export goods through Canning Port, since the over-silting of the river had made trade over waterways a difficult proposition. In 1868, the British constructed a fort at Chingrikhali, south of Diamond Harbour, to control the influx of pirates who had made a trade of selling the locals – both men and women – into slavery.

In 1897, Swami Vivekananda disembarked at Budge Budge ferry ghat, a town in the 24 Parganas district, on his return from the World Religion Conference at Chicago. The district was one of the larger geographical areas in Bengal, and had been divided into North and South, respectively, in 1896. The Sunderbans today falls under 24 Parganas South. Soon after Vivekananda's visit, Muslim ascetics wandered into the Sunderbans and started living in a part of the forestland. Thereafter, Hamilton arrived at Gosaba in 1903, and developed the village into a township, thereby influencing the way habitation thrived across the Indian Sunderbans.[3]

The residents on the various islands of the Sunderbans are a heterogeneous lot, a result of being ruled by several dynasties which brought about an eclectic mix of ideas, cultures and religions, plus a rich history of immigration, particularly in the post-Independence era. People have come to settle here because of various reasons, the promise of free farm land being a primary one. The continuous clearing of forests brought with it another set of problems: that of man-animal conflict.

About six months after my arrival, one evening, long after we had finished work for the day, for the first time, I heard firecrackers being burst in the vicinity of the campus. I dismissed them as a part of wedding celebrations or some other joyous occasion. The night watchmen, Guru-da and Sachin-da, came running from the main gate of the campus into the house and told me that I should not step out whatever the provocation. Realizing that I was clueless as to what was going on and why I was being instructed thus, they both went on to enlighten me: a tiger was in the vicinity.

When a tiger left its territory and ventured into inhabited land and the Forest Department got news of it – either through forest guards or through the villagers reporting a tiger sighting – they would burst firecrackers in the hope that the noise would scare the tiger back into his own territory. In a place where water kept changing boundaries, there was perhaps inevitability in tigers straying into human territory.

The Forest Department has supposedly built fencing around all the inhabited areas of the Sunderbans in an effort to mitigate unpleasant encounters of the natural world with mankind. This fencing is constantly monitored and maintained. However, entries by the villagers into forest areas to gather firewood and honey, and to fish, are daily occurrences. The fences have man-made breaches; sometimes water and wind damage them, too. Fishermen also cut passages for their boats to pass through. Tigers, being good swimmers, use these breaches to reach the villages.

Earlier, out of sheer ignorance and panic, the villagers would surround the tiger and kill it, exposing everyone involved to great danger. After years of publicity and spreading awareness about wildlife conservation, the villagers now cordon off the area where the tiger is spotted and inform the

Forest Department, who immediately send rescue teams to protect the villagers and capture the tiger. Over the years, the information network of the villagers and the effectiveness of the Forest Department have resulted in fewer deaths, of both man and animal. As soon as the villagers send word of a tiger sighting in a populated area, the Forest Department's rescue team arrives, armed with rescue kits, speedboats, tranquilizers and nets to capture the tiger. With the aid of villagers, the animal is captured and later released into the safety of the forest.

On the Indian side, the Directorate of Forest is responsible for the administration and maintenance of the Sunderbans National Park. It is headed by the principal chief conservator of forests. The Sunderbans Biosphere Reserve, headed by the chief conservator of forests, assisted by a deputy field director and an assistant field director, is responsible for the administration and maintenance at the local level. The Sunderbans National Park is divided into two ranges, overseen by range forest officers. Further, each range is subdivided into beats. It is to these beats that the villagers report any unusual wildlife activity. Also, throughout the park are several floating watch stations, camps and watchtowers to protect the forests and the wildlife therein from poachers. Plus, there is a considerable presence of the Indian and Bangladeshi naval forces in the open waters, demarcating the boundaries of the two nations.

The Bangladesh Sunderbans, which is double the size of the mangrove ecosystem on the Indian side, is spread across 5,770 sq. km, of which more than half is land, while the rest is covered by an intricate network of inter-connected water bodies. The region is defined by the Harinbhanga–Raimangal rivers on the west, the Baleshwar river on the east, the Bay of Bengal to the south, and land and human habitation along its northern boundary. 'For management purposes, the (Bangladesh) Sunderbans Reserved Forest has been divided into four zones: the *marine zone* to the extreme south; the *protection zone*, including the three wildlife sanctuaries, where no collection of forest produce is allowed; the *production zone*, that is regularly harvested and the *buffer zone*, comprising a 20 km belt on the periphery of the Reserved Forest.'[4]

However, the Bengal tiger respects no international boundaries and swims between India and Bangladesh. For most people visiting the Sunderbans, spotting a tiger is considered a sign of great luck. But for the locals, who, until very recently, depended solely on the forest for their survival – via honey-collecting, wood-gathering and fishing – not having an encounter with the tiger is a blessing! Because more often than not, a tiger chooses to come to a place inhabited by humans only when it doesn't find food in the forest – when it is hungry.

For many days after the bursting of firecrackers, the night

guards would announce every morning that they had heard the big cat roaring. Some of the villagers had even gathered on a few nights at the village embankment to assess the situation. However, the tiger chose not to make an appearance in our village.

The river embankments, encircling the villages, were reportedly built around the mid-19th century. Though put together without modern methods of construction, these embankments enabled permanent human settlements and made the mangrove forest relatively habitable. The embankments, when high and strong enough, are able to withstand tidal water and prevent it from entering the enclosed land, thereby rendering it salt free and, therefore, suitable for agriculture. However, even now, at times, strong tidal surges destroy significant portions of these *baandhs*, resulting in saline water gushing through and, sometimes over, the embankments and into agricultural fields, causing serious damage.

One morning towards the end of May, I woke up with strange marks all over my hands, face and neck. I was also feeling nauseated and dizzy. The minute the others saw me, they knew a poisonous spider had bitten me.

They urged me to take the matter seriously, because it was a huge health risk. The Sunderbans is home to many species of poisonous spiders and a spider bite can prove to be fatal. Since I didn't realize the import of it then, I tried to brush the matter aside by telling them not to worry. But they forced me to stay in bed. Mayna was instructed to give me as much fluids as possible, while Jogesh-da rushed to the forest to bring some medicinal herbs. By the time he returned from the forest, the nausea and dizziness had increased, and I was also feeling feverish. Mayna boiled the plants to make a concoction, and I bathed in that water. A small portion of the herbs was ground to a paste for me to ingest. Each morning, fresh herbs – both for oral consumption and bathing – were brought from and the forest and prepared. I followed this routine for almost an entire week. Due to high fever, I was delirious, and unaware of all that was happening around me. Though I didn't experience too much pain, the nausea and dizziness made the delirium worse. Jogesh-da told me later that for the first two days, the sickness was so severe and the fever so high that they were all very worried. Mayna stayed with me, ensuring I had plenty of fluids to drink and light meals. Going to the construction site was out of question, but Jogesh-da assured me that the workers were carrying on with utmost sincerity. Everyone in the village found out about my illness, and they were all very concerned. But Jogesh-da and the others didn't let anyone meet me, as I needed to rest. It was only after a week that I felt a slow and measured improvement, but the nausea and dizziness continued for well over a month.

In the light of this experience, the lack of healthcare of any grade or quality looked starker to me. This made me realize how imperative it was for the region to have a hospital of the kind the Foundation was constructing.

When the construction of the jetty was going on, a little girl, aged nine or ten, slipped on the jetty. She was playing with her friends when she fell from the platform on to the steps and broke her arm. She was rushed to a local quack who somehow set the bone and tied up the arm with what seemed like a bandage. Painkillers did not provide her much relief. Only when I insisted, quite aggressively, did the parents take the child to the Gosaba hospital so that the injury could be properly diagnosed and treated. The child, meanwhile, was wailing in pain.

The nearest hospital, on Gosaba Island, was at least two hours away by boat. Here, in the delta, distances are measured in hours rather than in kilometres. This distance proves fatal for many patients, particularly victims of snake bites and strokes. The government hospital anyway has limited facilities and infrastructure. For any specialized medical treatment, the locals need to go to Kolkata, a journey most patients cannot afford financially, and, in the case of a critical illness, in terms of time and distance, too. Private healthcare is out of the question.

In the Sunderbans, the creepy-crawlies are a part of everyday life. Snakes are common and scorpions are sighted very often. All night long, the lizards' *tik-tik, tik-tik* clicks ring out in the darkness, winning them the onomatopoeic name *tik-tikis*.

A group of volunteers from the Foundation were coming for a visit and Mayna was worried that one of the volunteers may wake up in the middle of the night to find a scorpion or a coiled up snake in the bathroom, or by the doorway. I asked her not to worry too much about the volunteers, who had been cautioned about the care they needed to take.

To help the volunteers understand the way of life in the Sunderbans, we organized a dinner for them where we also invited some of the local people. Chief amongst our guests was Anil Mistry, on whose ancestral land the Bali Nature Club is built. He was a former poacher and according to local lore, he once saw a doe and its baby grazing alongside in the mangroves and killed the mother. He saw tears of sorrow in the fawn's eyes, and had a change of heart. He now spends his days mostly in the forest, on his launch, tracking poachers and having them arrested. Very often, he travels to the Bangladesh side of the Sunderbans to meet with forest officials there to discuss how to keep the mangrove forests from further decline and to conserve what is left of them. A man with a strong social consciousness, he also runs various projects related to alternative livelihood opportunities and good governance in Bijaynagar. Anil-da and his colleague Colonel Banerjee, along with all the workers at the Bali Nature Club, had been instrumental in Samarpan Foundation establishing its base at Bali.

The following day, we took the volunteers on a visit to the mangrove forests. Their excitement was palpable as they all hopped on to Swapan-da's launch. One of them pointed to the fact that the tip of the launch was painted red. Swapan-da patiently explained that while red was the colour for danger – one was not supposed to step on to the red portion as it was too close to the water – it also symbolized the fact that the tip of the boat was sacred; it was worshipped to keep the boat safe from turbulent waters.

We disembarked at the Sajnekhali Forest Office to obtain entrance tickets to visit the forest, from which point a forest guide accompanied us. The Sajnekhali campus hosted a variety of birds, both local as well as migratory. Our next stop was the Sudhanyakhali Forest Office, which is known for its mangrove museum that displays over 80 species of mangroves. The guide, Paritosh-da, explained that based on their roots, mangroves were categorized into three types – stilt roots, knee-joint roots and snake roots. Taking a leisurely stroll around the forest office campus, we climbed on to the watchtower from where we spotted a few deer and a huge monitor lizard making its way across a creek, perhaps in pursuit of food. Though the forest was dense and the growth of the mangroves was thick, we were able to spot the animals due to the advantage of the height that we were at, and also because of clearings in the forest overgrowth. These are called observation lines; the Forest Department clears out small portions of the forest in order to do their work and to facilitate various studies related to observing the animals.

At the entrance of both Sajnekhali and Sudhanyakhali were small shrines dedicated to Bon Bibi, with a display board explaining her legend. At Sudhanyakhali, alongside this board was another board which gave details of the last tiger sighting. We had missed the evasive tiger by just two days! The animal had visited a fresh water pond created by the Forest Department precisely for tiger and other animal sightings and was spotted by the guards early in the morning. We said a little prayer to Bon Bibi to send the tiger our way, just close enough for us to observe the majestic animal, and also, of course, to protect us.

We passed through villages where women were standing knee-deep in water, trying to catch tiger-prawn seed, which would then be sold at the local markets. Of course, they were exposing themselves to immense danger in doing so; an attack by an estuarine crocodile could never be ruled out in the Sunderbans. At many places, there were thickets of *golpatta*, a variety of palm which is native to mangrove habitats. The leaves of the palm resemble the stripes of a tiger, and hence, it is said to be the favourite hide-out of the royal animal.

However, no amount of prayers and peeking into *golpatta* bushes resulted in a tiger sighting for us. It was late afternoon, and time for us to head back home. A delicious lunch of fish curry, dal, green vegetables and rice, which was cooked on the boat while we were traversing the forest, more than made up for the disappointment.

That evening, the Hare Rama Hare Krishna group came and sang for us. One of the singers' son, Palash, was working as a mason on our construction site. The locals call the members of this sect 'Vaishnavs', as they believe that Lord Vishnu is the beginning and end of this world. They pray to his avatars – Krishna and Rama. Their *bhakti* is particularly directed towards Krishna and his consort, Radha. While anyone can join this religious sect, they have to practise certain customs and respect some traditions. For example, while consumption of fish and meat is allowed, the members have to abstain from smoking. They wear a string of tulsi seeds – men around their wrists and women around their necks – to distinguish the Vaishnavs from the non-Vaishnavs.

The hardships of living in a place like the Sunderbans were perhaps eased by remembering the Lord's name. The harsh realities of life in the Sunderbans compel locals to follow rituals in the hope of protection. The sacred is woven into the mundane, even as the many myths that surround the region come alive in many little ways.

The Foundation's campus was teeming with patients who had started queuing up for the weekly clinic. One amongst them was Kailash Sahu, who had travelled all the way from faraway Ghoramara Island. He had brought along news that the island was shrinking; that the sea was engulfing it. Now, the village of Bijaynagar was buzzing; everyone was anxiously talking about how the sea was eating up the land of the Sunderbans.

The shifting of islands – even the complete disappearance of islands – is a very slow, yet alarming phenomenon, constantly taking place in the Sunderbans. The Lohachara Island, Suparibhanga or Bedford Island, Kabasgadi Island, Mousuni Island, and now, Ghoramara: these are islands which are fast disappearing due to rising sea levels. Research and satellite imagery have confirmed that over the last two decades, the water levels in the Sunderbans have risen at an average rate of 3.14 cm a year, which is much higher than the global average of 2 mm a year. Scientists are of the view that the sea level will rise up to a metre in the next 50 years, which will amount to a loss of 1,000 sq. km of land in the region[5]:

'...[Ghoramara island] has been reduced in size by 41 per cent since 1969, displacing 7,000 islanders over the past 30 years...the 3 km by 3 km piece of land that still offers shelter and sustenance to some 5,400 largely marginal farmers, fishermen and daily labourers, might not last beyond 2020... [I]n another 15 years the sea will lay claim to a dozen islands in the Sunderbans, six of which are populated, rendering about 70,000 people homeless.'[6]

Kailash Sahu was concerned about his entire island disappearing and the resultant disruption in the lives of thousands of inhabitants of Ghoramara – especially the loss of agricultural land owned by each family. He was of the opinion that although it was still relatively possible for families to shift from one island to another, and find a small piece of land to build a hut or even take up one on rent, it was near impossible to acquire a decent-sized piece of land for agricultural purposes. In such a case, it was very likely that all the grown-ups of the family would have to turn to daily-wage labour to earn money and the opportunities for labour work in the Sunderbans were few and far between.

As we waited for the team of doctors to arrive, Kailash-da also told us about another island that was fast disappearing. Sagara, 224.3 sq. km in area, has already lost 30 sq. km of its land to the sea. Research suggests that by 2020, it will have lost another 15 per cent, displacing more than 30,000 people. The reason for this conflict between land and water is the excessive amount of clearing of forest land to make space for human habitation. Naturally, this has put immense pressure on the ecosystem, leading to unnatural phenomenon like the rising levels of the sea.

In an attempt to save more arable land from disappearing into the sea, government authorities have tried to build massive embankments around islands which are under immediate threat. However, these efforts haven't proved very effective or useful, because during high tides, these embankments begin to give way, developing cracks and eventually collapsing.

It is estimated that other regions of coastal India face the same threat as the Sunderbans, and the loss of habitable land is already creating 'environmental refugees' – due to intra-regional as well as inter-regional migrations – who are thronging to cities in search of livelihood opportunities.[7] A report estimates that nearly one million people will become climate-change refugees by the year 2050. As preventive steps, the report suggests a planned retreat of humans from vulnerable areas and the planting of mangroves in those very same areas.[8]

On the one hand, climate change and rising sea levels challenge the long-term existence of the people in the delta; on the other, more basic and immediate existential challenges of poor infrastructure and depleting sources of livelihood persist. The Samarpan Foundation hospital intended to solve the issue of health in a small part of the delta. But we were beset with problems on the ground as the days went by. Apart from logistical concerns, there were also personal issues amongst workers that needed to be ironed out at times.

I had grown to rely on Mayna, Jogesh-da and Prateet-da as the construction progressed. Jogesh-da in particular was the prime mover-and-shaker in the village and on the site. We'd become comfortable enough with each other for him to express his opinions quite freely. It was to him that I turned each time there was a crisis. He had a strong backing from most of the workers on the site. So far, this had been working rather well, as I simply had to tell him what the task and target for each day was and he organized the workers accordingly.

However, a smaller group of workers had begun opposing Jogesh-da's decisions as overseer. They thought he had his chosen few whom he assigned less strenuous tasks to, while the rest had to do the heavy lifting. A man called Palash was the instigator. He and six other masons did not require work allocation by Jogesh-da as only the unskilled labour had to do different tasks each day. Their work varied between digging the ground, shifting construction material or lifting and moving heavy equipment or supplies from the delivery boats. It was here that differences began to arise, as some workers felt they were always assigned the toughest tasks. Palash, who had his own set of followers, had picked up on this thread of discontent and woven it into a story for malcontents.

The first two days of the casting of the roof of the hospital structure went by smoothly. On the third day, an argument started between Jogesh-da and Palash. They disagreed on the division of labour, and the way the work was being executed. What started as a squabble escalated quickly into a serious fight, with the workers ready to get into a physical altercation. Some of the onlookers also joined in, threatening to kill Palash for raising his voice against Jogesh-da.

I began to panic. The workers were simply not willing to listen to reason. Finally, I snapped at them that I had left behind a life of comfort to work on a hospital that was intended to bring relief to their lives. And that I had the option of turning around and leaving if they could not even be bothered to put aside their personal differences. The workers stood motionless. The concrete-mixing machine technicians turned off the machine's engine and as its noise slowly faded away there was an eerie silence. Just then, tea and snacks arrived and I left them to sort matters out amongst themselves.

When things cooled down, the others urged Jogesh-da and Palash to set aside their personal grudges and get on with work. The following morning, everyone went about their work as if nothing had happened. They seemed to have talked things over and it appeared the previous day's bickering was a thing of the past.

On the last day of roof-casting, Subroto, the carpenter on site and Jogesh-da's son, offered to sponsor tea and refreshments for everyone. He helped out with matters beyond the scope of his work and I had been fond of him since the beginning. I was touched by his offer. In a place where providing each meal could be a hard task, here was someone who wanted to feed us all. I tried to dissuade him but Subroto was adamant, and did exactly as he wanted.

Since the hospital now had a roof, we could begin work on the interiors. The floor of each room, as well as the corridors, would be tiled and the plastering of the walls could start. This was also the perfect time for setting up a drainage system, as we could check if it was functioning properly during the heavy monsoon season.

The monsoon arrived on time, in June. One day, wanting to make the most of a break that the rain clouds had taken, I decided to take a walk up to the jetty. There is a thumb rule in the Sunderbans during the time of monsoon: slippers, shoes and every kind of footwear has to be discarded. Everyone walked barefoot so as to avoid slipping in the slush. I did the same. As I got close to the jetty, I became concerned about the mudskippers and crabs populating the embankment area. I lost focus and slipped. With nothing to hold on to except the slush itself, I went skidding. My fall was broken by a part of the jetty wall that I hit with the full weight of my body.

Some of my neighbours were going about their chores around the jetty at that time and they saw me fall. They lifted me out of the slush and helped me back on my feet. The impact of the fall was so strong that my mobile phone had flown from my hands and was now buried somewhere in the depths of the Bidya river. As I was being taken home, covered in slush from head to toe, I became aware of the sharp pains and aches rising all over my body. My co-workers were understandably horrified to see me in that state. What followed was a lot of confusion and everyone fussing over me. After having a bath and using Mayna's phone to make a few calls, I decided to lie down because by then the pain was excruciating.

I had hurt my ribs, particularly on the left side. Once more, the absence of healthcare and medical assistance made matters worse. All I could do was rest and give in to the care and affection bestowed upon me by the people who had by now become my family. They patiently nursed me back to health over a period of one month.

In early July, perhaps the most beautiful time of the year, the monsoon had taken over almost every aspect of life in this wilderness. The sun would visit us briefly once every three or four days, because it was busy hiding behind a thick cloud cover. The landscape changed in a mere two weeks. As we moved from June to July, the surroundings turned from a predominantly dry brown to a lush green. Dried-up ponds slowly came back to life. The greenery was complemented by red, yellow, orange, pink, lavender and white flowers blooming, on creepers, bushes and trees.

This was also the time to sow paddy. Since people worked in collectives, the nearby families got together to work on their individual lands, one after the other. The land needed to be tilled first. While the relatively affluent could afford to hire a mechanized tiller, many still used the traditional *hal* (yoke and plough) with two bullocks pulling at it across the length and breadth of the fields. Later in the year, I would realize that there were very few families in the Sunderbans who could afford a second paddy crop. While in places like Ladakh, the reason for not being able to sow a second crop in the same year was the harsh and unsuitable weather conditions, in the Sunderbans, the reason was lack of water for irrigational purposes. The river water is salty, and thereby only nourishes mangroves and their associates. Only those families who have the money to arrange for non-saline water for irrigation are able to sow a second round of paddy in the forest of tides. Water forms an inalienable part of lives in this delta. Though it takes lives, it is also essential for sustenance and for agriculture. There is presence of brackish water in most places, but it is as unsuitable for cultivation as it is for anything else. The only source of non-saline water is rain water which is delivered in torrents during the monsoon. The concept of rainwater harvesting is unknown to the locals. Even if it were introduced, there would be the issue of the collected water getting salinated due to a very high salt content in the groundwater.

As the landscape changed with the season, so did the winds' direction and strength. Now was the time for the southerly winds and they are very strong; it also meant that the waters became choppy and there was immense roiling, making it unsafe to travel by boats. Practically, this meant that the locals did not commute even within the Sunderbans unless absolutely necessary. In comparison to the time of the northerly winds, when the surface of the waters is very calm and the weather is dry and pleasant, this time of the year was also extremely humid.

I began to judge the safety of travel by assessing the sky and I couldn't help contrast this to my view of the sky in the city... Unlike the city skyline, where one's vision was limited and constrained, in the Sunderbans, one could see until the horizon. It was a visual delight to observe the distant cloud formation, and the ever-changing sky above the layers of water and mangroves.

On the one hand, there is the remoteness from what is called 'civilization' and lack of any infrastructure worth the name. On the other hand, the question bothered me whether improvements in the health and education infrastructure would attract more settlers and end up in overpopulating the fragile delta. But I could not dwell much on such thoughts; the needs of the people had an urgency and immediacy – it was a question of survival. If one does not survive today, how does one think of tomorrow, let alone a year or a few decades ahead? For me, helping alleviate the daily struggle for survival by the locals was of paramount importance. A future possibility of overpopulation was something I chose to leave out of the ambit of my worries.

# Mangroves

—

## The Forest and Livelihoods

After about seven months of living in the Sunderbans, in August, I had begun craving for 'home'. A feeling of melancholy had enveloped me. There were days when I woke up with a particularly strong yearning to 'belong' somewhere. On one such difficult morning, I woke up to the chirping of birds long before dawn. Thoughts of that lone heron struggling to get to safety during the cyclone came to my mind. Where was home for this beautiful bird with its slender neck and long, delicate legs? Had it managed to reach the safety of its home and reunite with its family? Do hermit crabs feel unsettled by their constant moving of homes? Perhaps not. I presume birds and animals must be adapting to nature instinctively and more harmoniously than human beings do, and are never in conflict with it. Take the weaver bird families, for instance. They had chosen to weave their nests on the Foundation's campus: on the *taal* tree, the Asian Palm, but only on the male tree. The female tree bears the delicious, pulpy *taal* fruit which is also used to brew local liquor – a frailty of the local men and a nuisance for the women because the men get addicted to it. To me, it tasted bitter and acidic and had a pungent smell.

I was fascinated by the skill and artistry of the weaver birds. Their nests, woven with fibres of grass, are nothing less than a work of art. The *bayas*, as weaver birds are locally known, are also called *shilpi pakhi,* or 'sculptor birds'. Their nests are spherically suspended, with some variations between the one that the male bird initially builds to woo a female and the one in which the female lays her eggs. According to the locals, each year before weaving their nests, the birds are intuitively able to sense the direction from which there will be maximum rainfall, and the nest (which has two entrances at the bottom) is built in a way to shield it from the rain. Several nests are built one next to the other as a colony on the same branch of a single tree, presumably for better protection in numbers. An Asian Palm tree close to a water body is the preferred choice of the *bayas*.

In the mangrove forests of the Sunderbans, all animals hold a significant place in local folklore. In a region where the distinction between land and water is not always apparent, the protection of gods is called upon at all times. Creation and destruction are often concurrent and keep happening constantly. As land and water merge to create mudflats, especially at deltaic islands and at estuaries, where the rivers meet the tides, huge deposits of silt sometimes create new islands. Where this geological activity is minimal, mangroves take roots. And like everything in the delta, they, too, are said to have mythical abilities.

In the delta, where saltwater barely allows plants to survive, mangroves thrive in high salinity areas and deal with the twice-a-day submergence in tidal waters. Some species are aided in this by salt-secreting glands in their leaves. Some mangroves that grow away from the shore have a bushy growth, and even though they can withstand salt and tides, their tolerance is not as high as true mangroves. There are 84 species of 'true mangroves, mangrove-associates and back mangroves found in the Sunderban mangrove forest. However, the distribution of species is not uniform and [is] primarily controlled by the level of salinity and not by the tidal inundation,'[1] says a report by the West Bengal Forest Department.

For the uninitiated, a mangrove forest can be an optical illusion, to put it mildly. Viewing it from the safety of the deck of a launch, it seems alluring, almost welcoming. The mangrove tree tops seem like any other regular tree tops – dense, green and comforting. On a closer look, one finds colourful berries and flowers; the berries of a few species are poisonous. The leaves closer to the water have coatings of salt deposit, the salt brought in by the tides as they rise and fall. This makes the leaves appear to have two different shades of green – the lower half a lighter green from this coating, and the upper half is relatively darker, which is the natural colour.

The same mangroves appear very different when their roots are exposed as the tides recede. Camouflaged and quite at home within the roots are insects, animals and birds. It seems like an apparition – the mix of brown roots and green leaves – rising from the waters and stretching unto the horizon.

My maiden launch trip had brought me into the Sunderbans, from Godkhali. Over the course of my stay, I went deeper into the forest of tides to visit different islands to explore, and in the hope of sighting the elusive tiger. Stories I had heard, and legends I had been told, turned my initial wonderment about the majestic-looking forests into feelings of awe-filled fear and reverence. But as I allowed the forests to grow on me, the feeling of awe passed and I started to feel protected and sheltered.

Human settlement here in the past few centuries has led to environmental imbalance and serious ecological threats such as disturbances in the natural food chain, an alarming decrease in wildlife population, coastal erosion, decreasing soil fertility and increasing occurrence of storms and cyclones. One such depredation by humans is the extensive cutting down of trees to meet demands for firewood, and for timber to build houses, furniture and boats. The large-scale felling of mangrove trees has led to soil erosion and the weakening and washing away of large areas of embankments. Logging, together with clearing of mangrove swathes for habitation and agricultural land, has eventually led to the exposure of people and land to natural disasters like storms and cyclones. Mangroves also act as natural sewage management plants and tend to absorb pollutants from both air and water. Diminishing numbers of these special varieties of flora can lead to serious natural impediments especially when combined with the fact that there are plans to set up international waterways, oil refineries and other projects to 'develop' the region.

But the Sunderbans is more than just an undeveloped natural resource for those who live here. For locals, everything that lives and grows in the delta has significance. Alternating every six hours, the tide rushes in to meet the land and then retreats back to the ocean. Depending on the waning and waxing of the moon, water levels can rise and fall anywhere between 15–20 feet! For someone who has never visited the Sunderbans or experienced the majestic magnitude of the mangroves and the games played by the high and low tides, it is virtually impossible to imagine what goes on inside the depths of the mangrove forests. During high tide, all creatures, big and small, are forced to move inland to the area that is not submerged. From crabs to snakes to crocodiles to tigers, Mother Nature forces them all to come together, face-to-face, and co-exist until the waters recede. And when humans enter into this very congregation of wildlife for their livelihood and sustenance – to gather wood, honey, fruit, crabs, etc. – they have to respect these creatures.

Folklore dominates the life of the people here. There is a pantheon of gods with one each for every separate aspect of life – deities to be respected, feared and worshipped. Makal Thakur and Biswalakshmi are the deities of fish; Olabibi is worshipped for protection against cholera; Sitala is the goddess to whom one prays for remission from smallpox and measles. Then there's Bisalakshi, a tribal mother goddess and a tantric deity; Ateshwar, the protector of the forests who guarantees the safety of the inhabitants of the Sunderbans as well as of their domestic animals; Jorasur, who cures fevers; and Jagatguru, who prevents cobra bites. Devi Tusu, the goddess of fertility, is also worshipped as a goddess of harvest. She is popular amongst the aboriginals of the Sunderbans, and is an ancient tribal deity who is also worshipped in areas outside the delta as well.

Every deity has his or her own myth which extols his or her powers. One of the demi-gods, Bada Gazi Khan – a preacher said to have supernatural powers – chose the delta rather than his own father's kingdom as his fief. He rides a horse and is credited with saving children from the many dangers of the delta and preserving livestock. His adopted brother, Kalu Rai, who walked out on the kingdom and followed him into the delta, protects people from crocodile attacks. Manik Pir, who protects cattle, grew up in abject poverty and chose to be a mendicant. He wandered from village to village in the company of his brother. One day, he arrived at the home of a wealthy Hindu merchant whose wife refused to give him anything to eat. The daughter-in-law of the merchant took pity on the fakir and offered him food and milk. In return, he granted her the boon of being able to milk endless pots of milk from her cows.

Some deities, like Bhangar Pir, are also known all over the state. Bhangar Pir was a powerful Islamic preacher during the medieval period after whom the popular Bhangar market and the Bhangar West Bengal Vidhan Sabha Kendra are named. His shrine is next to an ancient banyan tree which, according to botanists, is over a thousand years old. According to legend, during the Pir's annual *urs*, tiny orange flowers bloom for one night, withering away at dawn. Naturally, his *mazaar* is a popular pilgrimage centre, not just for Muslims but also for Hindu devotees, all year round.

There is a likelihood that, in the churn that has happened over time, names of the deities who figure in the folklore have changed from Hindu to Muslim and vice versa. In a land where Hindus and Muslims both have to face the same threats to their lives, the syncretism that has evolved and is unique to this forest of tides was perhaps inevitable. A good example of this syncretism are the shrines built for Bon Bibi. In Hindu-dominated villages in the Sunderbans, she is portrayed as a feminine figure dressed in a saree and finery including a crown and garlands, riding a tiger or a crocodile, with a child on her lap. Her Hindu worshippers worship her as Bandevi or Bandurga. The Muslim portrayal depicts her with braided hair, dressed in traditional Muslim feminine attire (instead of a saree), with a cap and shoes, and worship her as Banbibi or Pirani.

However, the rituals followed in her worship by both communities are the same. Wild flowers, creepers, certain weeds and seeds picked from the forest are offered to her as a mark of respect and to show that the communities are committed towards saving the forests. Interestingly, the goddess Manasa is depicted by both communities as a woman covered with snakes, either sitting on a lotus or standing upon a snake. She is sheltered by a canopy of hoods of seven cobras. Sometimes, she is depicted with a child on her lap, who is assumed to be Astika, her son.

The narratives of Bon Bibi are found in texts called *Banbibir Keramati* (*The Magical Deeds of Banbibi*) and the *Banbibir Jahuranama* (*Glory to Banbibi*). These texts shed light on two specific chronicles: her battle with Dakshin Rai and the story of Dukhe. The Bengali folk epic *Manasamangal* – the life story of goddess Manasa – has portions of it set in the Sunderbans where Behula met the washerwoman, Nethi, and was eventually successful in bringing her husband Lokhinder, the son of Chand Sadagar, back to life. These legends dominate the everyday lives of those who live here amid the mangrove forests.

I first met Basanti when she had come for a check-up at the Thursday medical camp. Basanti had come to Bijaynagar as a young bride of 15 from Mollakhali, an island four hours away from Bali. It was easy to spot her in her colourful sarees at the village markets, haggling with the grocer, or chatting incessantly with the women who would gather at the tube well to fill water. Her feisty nature was endearing. She remembered coming to her husband's village in a *bhotbhoti*, hired to transport the wedding guests. Her father owned large tracts of land in Mollakhali. Apart from growing their own crop of paddy and potatoes, the family also leased out land to others. Basanti had had limited interaction with the forest and was unaware of its rules until her marriage to Bhabho, who collected honey and firewood from the forest. To support her new family, she had to work as a tiger-prawn seed collector. This meant spending long hours in the waters with her nets spread far and wide, and exposing herself to wildlife attacks.

Basanti told me that when her in-laws first suggested that she should learn to catch tiger-prawn seed, she was nonplussed. Largely because she didn't know what was required of her. When the process was explained to her, the confusion metamorphosed into anxiety. She couldn't fathom how she would manage to stand knee-deep in water for hours at a stretch. What if she needed to relieve herself; and what would happen during her menstrual cycle? I could almost imagine Basanti, the petite child-bride's eyes becoming large and luminous with fear. However, this was not a choice; she had no voice in the matter. There were no options – what had to be done had to be done. Her neighbours, who were adept at the job, gently initiated her into the physically draining and tedious process. While reminiscing about her initial days as a tiger-prawn seed collector, Basanti was most amused and couldn't stop laughing at her initial apprehensions and meekness.

Having grown up as a landowner's daughter, she had witnessed, first-hand, how discrimination happened, based on what people have and did not have. While she, too, had to work on her family's land, she was secure in the knowledge that she was working on what was her own. The land would provide for them, no matter what. 'As a child, I used to look down on those who did not own land and had to rent land from my father,' she told me.

But her smugness quickly turned to humility when she came to Bijaynagar and saw that her husband's family was dependent on the forest. On the small patch of land that they owned, they grew their annual stock of paddy and potatoes, but that was not nearly enough. Basanti's husband had to go into the forest to catch fish and crabs and to gather firewood and honey, to be sold to provide for the family of eight – Basanti and her husband, their three children, her husband's parents and his younger sister. To support her husband in providing for the family, she began to collect tiger-prawn seed. The tiger prawn, a marine crustacean, is reared for food and is considered a delicacy by many. The spawn of these prawns, called seed, is collected from the waters and sold to fisheries to be hatched, reared and sold in the seafood markets. If a seed collector manages to catch hatchlings along with the seed, these young shrimps are bred in their own ponds and then sold once they mature into giant tiger prawns.

Living in the Sunderbans, one can never be rid of the thought of being attacked by a tiger. In Basanti's case, this thought – of a tiger attack, either on herself or her husband – was emphasized as their survival was dependent on the forest. In her case, she also feared a crocodile attack. She had heard unnerving, graphic stories of how the crocodile grabbed its victims, dived with them underwater, thrashed about till they died and then ate them. The initial trepidation of her in-laws, about their son going away to the forest and the anxiety associated with waiting for him to return, had mellowed over time. In comparison, since Basanti had to only go to the nearby river, they were not as perturbed by her exposure to the risks. While Basanti's children took all this in their stride, accepting it as a way of life, they were wary – as much about their father's safe return from the forest as their mother's from the river. None of them wanted to follow in their parents' footsteps. Basanti's deepest desire was for them to study well, go away to the city and make a successful life for themselves. 'I want them to work out of an office,' she said. She herself, though, was glad that she could collect tiger-prawn seed in her spare time; this had made her economically independent.

Basanti told me the forest never differentiates between people. Whether it is the haves or have-nots, whether it is Hindus or Muslims, whether it is men or women – they are all the same once they go into the forest. Everyone receives from the bounty of Mother Nature; everyone is prone to wildlife attacks; and everyone prays to Ma Bon Bibi in their hour of distress.

Basanti patiently explained to me what her work entailed. A group of four or five women went to the river together, both for company during the long and arduous work hours, and for security. In case one of them came under attack, the others could fetch help, she elaborated. Though I couldn't help wondering at the futility of this. Mostly, they went to the closest river bank suitable for their work. At times, if they had a boat at their disposal, or if one of the men had some time to spare, he would accompany them deeper into the forest, or to the confluence of two or more rivers, where they could get a better catch. They entered the river until the waters came to their chests and cast their nets. If on foot, they would pull the nets behind them as they walked back to the shore. 'We even expose ourselves to attacks by sharks, crocodiles and tigers,' she remarked casually.

She went on to tell me the story of the tragedy that had befallen Guru-da's wife, who had gone to the river to gather prawn seed. She, along with three other women, were deep in the river and had just started pulling at their nets when a crocodile emerged from the depths of the water and caught hold of her. The other women ran for their lives, and by the time they reached their homes and alerted the men, the crocodile had pulled the woman deep under water. Guru-da, along with other men from the neighbourhood, spent hours looking for her, but in vain. 'They could not even find his wife's body to give her a decent burial. She was gone, just like that,' Basanti spoke, her hands, eyes and tone all part of how she expressed herself. 'Despite all this, if we are lucky and get a good catch, it usually means that our families can eat well for the next few days,' she said.

Basanti also enlightened me on the gender roles within the local communities. Although the men treated women as equals when they worked outside the house, at the end of the day, the women were still expected to light the kitchen fire and feed the family, no matter how hard the day might have been. The men didn't help with the cooking, even though their working conditions were the same. 'But I am not complaining,' she said animatedly. 'Things could be worse. We work hard, and somehow make ends meet. I have no issues with my in-laws; they adore me. My husband, too, cares for me. Yes, it would be nice to be able to buy a few sarees for myself, but as long as I can buy a set of new clothes for the children every year for Durga Puja, I can make-do with my old sarees. At least I can afford to buy new glass bangles every few months,' she smiled, as if to reassure me.

'Then there are all these relations we form as part of our work. We women, who step into the water together, look out for each other. We have each other's backs, as far as possible. We share not only food and the imminent dangers associated with our work, but also everyday issues like whether there is enough firewood in the other's house or not. Maybe our relations with our co-workers, who are mostly our neighbours, would not be so strong if not for the fact that we are, to a great extent, dependent on each other for our safety,' Basanti added.

The meeting with Basanti made me realize kinship and community relations were far more important in the delta than elsewhere. Perhaps there is a greater sense of responsibility and friendship towards those in one's proximity than with those with whom one has familial relations. While male friends referred to each other as *bandhu*, female friends are addressed as *bandhavi* or *soi*, the latter having its origin in the friendship between Bon Bibi and Narayani Devi, Dakshin Rai's mother. Like most things in the delta, even friendships are protected by the gods.

Magic, totems and animism play important roles in the religious practices of the Sunderbans. So does the worship of forests, rivers and animals. This worship is firmly rooted in the belief that natural objects and phenomena have souls as well. The most intriguing evidence of this belief is the tiger charmer: *bauley* or *bawali*.

On most days, Bapi Naskar can be found tending to his rice fields in Bijaynagar, running errands for the panchayat, facilitating meetings between the forest office staff and the locals, or fishing and collecting firewood. But there are days when he is called upon for his skills as a tiger charmer: to protect others from the delta's most elusive and yet most fearsome beast.

The tiger is never referred to by its name. Instead, he is always referred to as fakir by the Muslims and *mamu* by the Hindus. It is considered an ill omen if a tiger is referred to as a tiger. Bapi's job as a tiger charmer begins when a launch full of people – wood-cutters, fishermen, honey-gatherers, tourists, forest officials – visit the mangrove forests. When the boat halts, Bapi disembarks first from the boat and places his palm on Mother Earth. If the hand begins to shake, there is a tiger somewhere in the area. Only when the hand stops to shake is it safe for the others to get off the boat and enter the forest.

'Bon Bibi and, at times, Dakshin Rai, the lord of tigers himself, visit the chosen ones amongst us in our dreams. They teach certain charms to certain people to help them ward off dangers in the forest,' Bapi told me. 'I was 20 when Dakshin Rai, riding a huge tiger, appeared to me in my dream. He spoke to me and said he had a special task for me to do. He taught me a few charms and said I was to maintain a balance between man and tiger and avoid a conflict at all costs. He also said I was never to speak of or discuss the charms.' Bapi was almost breathless as he recounted his initiation as a tiger charmer.

After Dakshin Rai had said what he had to, Bapi saw Bon Bibi appearing by the tiger god's side and smiling benevolently at Bapi. When he woke up in the morning, Bapi thought he had been hallucinating. He feared that if he told anyone about his dream, people would laugh at him and say that he had lost his mind. Eventually, unable to restrain himself any longer, he told his elder brother. The man was jubilant and Bapi could not understand why. Only when he explained to Bapi the significance of the dream and the fact that Bapi was now the chosen one, did Bapi fully comprehend his good luck.

Bapi spoke to me at length about the mysterious and mystical ways of a tiger charmer. 'Depending on the attitude of the tiger in question, our approach is either meek or bold, and this is completely our prerogative,' he explained. As I understood, both men and women could be tiger charmers, but once they have been initiated into this field where divinity crosses over to real life, they have to adhere strictly to the rules. People who are monied or own land cannot go into the forest, either as tiger charmers or to gather resources. Only those who are poor and depend on the generosity of the forest to survive, can enter the forest.

Tiger charmers also have to be free from the divisions of caste, religion and gender, genuinely believing in the universal concept of Oneness and must treat everyone as an equal. Emphasizing this fact, even troupes that enact the life story of Bon Bibi feature actors from all castes and communities. For tiger charmers, the reason for going into the forest has to be selfless, i.e. to protect people from tigers, and not personal gain. They have to enter with a *'pabitro mon'*, or pure heart, and *'khali haatey'*, or empty hands. They cannot take more than what is absolutely necessary. The idea behind this is also to enter the forest with the simplicity and innocence of Dukhe – whose story is recounted in detail below – and with absolute faith in Bon Bibi's protective powers.

What applies on land does not necessarily apply to the forest: it has its own set of rules. It is inhabited by non-humans and its resources are to be shared by all. Furthering the belief that the forest has its own rules, the shrines built in honour of the lady of the forest are never built on anyone's private property. They are all on community land or on common pathways used by everybody, and, of course, within the forest itself. Since the locals believe Bon Bibi was sent by Allah to protect the people of the Sunderbans from the demon Dakshin Rai, tiger charmers do not enter the forest on a Friday, *jumma*; they do not eat crab or pork; and they do not lend or borrow money on interest.

Folks like Bapi don't call themselves 'tiger charmers' either; they prefer to remain servants of Bon Bibi. 'We are no different from the others who go into the forest as and when the need arises. Sometimes, we venture deep into the forest waters to catch crabs and fish, which we sell to make a living. At other times, we delve into the depths of the mangrove forests to collect honey and to gather wood, again for self-sustenance. But when we go into the forests as tiger charmers, our approach is simply to make sure that humans avoid meeting non-humans. We also ascertain that those who go to gather resources from the forest only take as much as is needed, without getting greedy. At times, when we feel that the might of the tiger may work more than our charms, we get folks to cancel their trips.'

The locals, and especially teams from the Forest Department, consider it an absolute necessity to be accompanied by one of the charmers when visiting the forests. Tiger charmers are also believed to be able to control storms and cure illnesses, particularly those related to the forest.

Since they mediate between humans and tigers, tiger charmers have to ensure that one is not a threat to the other. An important part of their job is to persuade folks not to disturb wildlife. The best time to visit the forest is either in the morning or the afternoon, when the animals are not hunting for prey. According to Bapi, these are the times when they rest. In return for this respect, the animals do not harm humans when the latter are in their territory. As a rule, tiger charmers do not accompany poachers and fishermen who endeavour to collect prawn seed. Since both prawn seed collection by men and poaching are activities that are done at night, and out of sheer greed, tiger charmers find the practices unethical and refuse to protect those involved.

When Bapi checks the ground for the presence of a tiger in the vicinity, he also asks for forgiveness from the forest and from Mother Earth for disturbing their equilibrium and for partaking of their resources. This courtesy is extended to the tigers thanking them for understanding the need for humans to trespass into their territory. Equally important is the ritual of undoing the charms when leaving the forest. A slow bow of the head signals the completion of the visit.

Interestingly, one school of thought in the Sunderbans has it that the tiger charmers are descendants of fakirs, who were amongst the first settlers in the Sunderbans. Perhaps this legend has its origin from the pirs who were said to possess magical powers; they used their abilities to heal people and to reorient them towards spirituality. It is believed that these pirs were also able to control the wild beasts of the forests, especially the big cat, with the aid of their magic. Then the question arises how are there Hindu tiger charmers, like Bapi Naskar? Religious lines in the Sunderbans, especially in the yesteryears, were never drawn very strictly and conversions were not uncommon (though without the drama, fundamentalism, and fanaticism associated with the act today).

Listening to Bapi's description of his job was fascinating.

However, if anybody can invoke Bon Bibi and seek her protection against attacks from wildlife and other dangers in the forest, why does one need a tiger charmer at all? The village elders told me that fishermen or crab-catchers go into the forest for a relatively smaller booty as compared to wood-cutters and honey-gatherers. The need for the latter to appease the tiger and the forest he lives in was far greater than that of the former as they would be encroaching on tiger territory more than the fishermen. Hence, the tiger charmers play a pivotal, peace-making role between man and nature.

'Tiger-charmers are expected to be humble and peaceful so as to be in accordance with Bonbibi's wishes and yet, at times, arrogant and violent so as to stand up to greedy Dokkhin [Dakshin] Rai and those tigers who emulate him. It is tiger-charmers who decide in each specific situation the stance to adopt – whether meekness or defiance – to smooth potential disagreements between the two groups.'[2]

But when I asked the same elders about the effectiveness of tiger charmers in today's world, their opinions were divided. Some said that 'charms and charmers' sounded good when telling tales about the Sunderbans, but when faced by a tiger, no man or woman would risk their lives for others. To take responsibility for whether it was safe for a group of people to enter the forest at a particular time or not was not everyone's cup of tea. It required a lot of strength of character as well as conviction. Like everything else in the Sunderbans, tiger charmers, too, are a matter of absolute faith.

In the Sunderbans, the cult of Bon Bibi is all pervasive. She is the one whom everyone prays to. The other deities are worshipped with fervour, but it is Bon Bibi who stands tall as the guardian deity of the forests and the delta.

The legend of Bon Bibi begins with the story of Dukhe, which is often performed as a *pala*, or a *jatra*: a folk performance. In the village of Barijhati lived two brothers, Dhanai and Manai (nicknamed Dhona and Mona), who made a living by collecting honey from the forest. One day, Dhona wanted to go deep into the forest to gather honey with an expedition of seven boats. Mona opposed this plan because it was dangerous to venture too far into the land of eighteen tides. Dhona managed to convince his brother and they set out with seven boats. Along with the boatmen, they took their nephew, a young boy named Dukhe, who lived with his widowed mother. Dukhe, whose name means the miserable one, was aptly named. The boy was always sad; his cries could be heard from afar, even when he was a baby. Dukhe and his mother lived in abject poverty. So when his uncles suggested that they would take care of their young nephew and feed him well on the forest trip, Dukhe's mother could not refuse and with heavy heart, she sent Dukhe. She instructed him to call out to Ma Bon Bibi if he were to find himself in any trouble.

As a tradition, anyone who visits the forests has to make an offering to appease the demon king, Dakshin Rai, the lord of the south. Those who enter the mangrove forests without making an offering are attacked by Dakshin Rai in the guise of a tiger. But Dhona and Mona forgot to pay their homage to the demon king, and they could not gather any honey for three days. On the third night, Dakshin Rai appeared in Dhona's dream and reminded him of his impropriety. As compensation, the brothers were asked to make a human sacrifice.

Finding themselves in a peculiar situation, the brothers decide to offer the unsuspecting Dukhe as a sacrifice. Accepting the offer, the demon king allowed Dhona and Mona to fill all their boats with precious honey. In return, the brothers had to leave Dukhe on the banks of Kedokhali Island and return to their village.

When the brothers left Dukhe on Kedokhali Island, Dakshin Rai was waiting in the form of a tiger. Dukhe, realizing what had transpired between his uncles and Dakshin Rai, was despondent. Just when he was about to be devoured by the tiger, he remembered his mother's advice. He frantically started chanting the name of Bon Bibi, invoking her divine protection. On hearing Dukhe's desperate cry for help, Bon Bibi arrived with her twin brother, Shah Jongoli, who took on Dakshin Rai in a fierce battle and defeated him.

Dakshin Rai was forced to take refuge with Bada Gazi Khan, the well-wisher and caretaker of the people of the Sunderbans. When Bon Bibi and Shah Jongoli followed him there, Dakshin Rai pleaded his case with the three deities. He told them that the people had stopped paying their respects and making food offerings to him and so he had to resort to such evil ways. Bada Gazi Khan intervened and requested the brother–sister duo to spare Dakshin Rai's life. He also forced Dakshin Rai to apologize to Bon Bibi for his transgression – for preying upon those who seek her protection.

There is a further backstory to this. Bon Bibi had previously engaged with Dakshin Rai's mother, Narayani, in a great war. Dakshin Rai was once a great sage who meditated in these forests. But the constant intrusion of locals into the forests to collect wood or honey disturbed his meditation. In a fit of great anger, he vowed to feed on them. Using his ascetic powers, he transformed himself into a ferocious tiger, claiming rights over the forest, refusing to share any of its resources with humans. He crowned himself king of not just the delta, but also of all the tigers, spirits, gods and demons that lived within it. Over time, he turned into a demon himself, disrupting the equilibrium and peace between man and nature.

Scared for their lives, the people prayed to their protectors and preservers: Bon Bibi and her brother Shah Jongoli. They built shrines for them in the forest and in their villages. As a result, Bon Bibi started protecting people from Dakshin Rai's attacks, making the demon king furious. When the sound of one such prayer reached Dakshin Rai's ears, he sent his friend, Sanatan Rai, to find out what was happening. When Sanatan informed him about the duo, he decided to take on Bon Bibi in battle and oust the siblings from his territory.

Dakshin Rai's mother, Narayani, intervened and calmed him down. She explained that only a woman could take on Bon Bibi in battle. She offered to do so on her son's behalf, with her army of ghosts and goblins, and asked him to fight Shah Jongoli instead. A great, long battle ensued in the delta: between Bon Bibi and Narayani Devi and Dakshin Rai and Shah Jongoli. All four fought bravely, but the brother–sister duo eventually defeated the mother and son. Narayani fell at the feet of Bon Bibi, seeking forgiveness and asking her to spare their lives. Bon Bibi embraced Narayani, addressing her as *soi*, or sister. The two became close allies and Bon Bibi ensured that people worshipped not just her but also Narayani. While the inhabited part of the Sunderbans was kept under Bon Bibi and Shah Jongoli's protection, Bon Bibi returned half of Dakshin Rai's kingdom, including the deep forests, to the mother and son. Since then, the word '*soi*' is used to signify close bonds between women in rural Bengal.

But by attacking Dukhe, Dakshin Rai had broken his pact with Bon Bibi. Dukhe's pleas warmed the mother goddess's heart and it was decided that while Bada Gazi Khan would give him several precious items, Dakshin Rai would give him many boatloads of honey and wax from the forests. In return, Bon Bibi and Shah Jongoli would not harm Dakshin Rai and he would continue to be worshipped by the people venturing into his forests. Bon Bibi's pet crocodile, Seko, was instructed to accompany Dukhe on his journey back home to his mother. Once back in the village, Dukhe built a shrine for Bon Bibi. Dhona married off his daughter, Champa, to Dukhe, who was later elected as the head of the village and lived a life of abundance with his mother and wife, under the protection and guidance of Bon Bibi.

Bon Bibi is an inseparable part of the people of the forest of tides. Even as she protects humans, she also shelters the beasts of the forests. She stands for everything that is just and right. 'For the islanders, Bon Bibi goes against the distinctions of caste, class and religion. This is the reason why those who work in the forests as fishers and crab-collectors stress the fact that they have to consider all *jatis* – whether Brahmin or Malo, rich or poor, Hindu or Muslim, or even human or animal – "equal".'[3]

The feeling of melancholy that had come over me quite suddenly hung over me like a cloud refusing to lift. It was affecting my work, too. The ills of working in a patriarchal and rural society had started to emerge slowly after my first meeting with the panchayat at Kalitola, where we were accused of cutting down mangroves. We would often get strange requests from them to co-opt a certain person into the work force, or their emissaries, who came to the campus on the pretext of conducting inspections, to be fed and entertained.

Then a worker from the construction site began to follow me on my walks, trying to strike up a conversation. After being polite on a few occasions, I began to avoid him, even though I did not perceive his over-friendliness as a threat. The matter reached the ears of the panchayat, who summoned me once again to warn me against my 'indecent behaviour'! I was told not to encourage the village youth to behave in an unacceptable manner. I stormed out of their office, but not before giving them a piece of my mind. I did not dismiss the worker, as the panchayat had instructed me to do. The fact that I stood my ground did not go down very well with them.

On another occasion, while the construction was in full swing, the panchayat sent a message that the Foundation needed to pay something called 'party fees' to continue with the construction. This was unfamiliar vocabulary to me. When

I narrated this to Jogesh-da the following morning, the range of emotions that crossed his face showed that all was not well. He explained to me gently that it was a covert request for a bribe.

A meeting was arranged later that evening at a panchayat worker's house. I went with Jogesh-da and Panchu-da, my trusted aides, who had requested me to let them do the talking, at least initially. Two panchayat members were already there when we reached the venue. In a roundabout way, which is the norm of such negotiations, both sides tried to put their views across. We suggested that the hospital was for the community's benefits and that it was the panchayat's responsibility to not just encourage and support the initiative, but also to ensure that there were no hurdles. The two members jumped at this and said that was why they were demanding 'party fees', so that any hurdles in the form of permissions not being granted or licenses and other paperwork being stuck etc., could be taken care of. I couldn't help but intervene at that point. I was livid at this grotesque display of a culture of bribery. I said in no uncertain terms that the demand was shameful. A heated argument followed, after which I chose to walk out. Over the course of a week, I realized the futility of taking the moral high ground, grudgingly decided to be pragmatic, and finally gave in. One had to accede to such demands in the interest of the greater good of the masses, was the explanation I received.

Was that the reason for my melancholy? That I had realized the Sunderbans may hold immense beauty, but it also held within it the same greed of human beings prevalent everywhere else? Perhaps.

As much as I was engulfed by conflicting feelings arising out of these unpleasant dealings, the delta had embraced me with a tranquillity I had rarely known. As dawn broke amid the chattering of the *bayas*, everything else also came alive: pink, white and blue lotuses opened their petals to the world amid the slush and brackish water and the rice fields appeared to welcome the farmers who returned to them day after day.

One morning, I sat watching the arrival of dawn and the colours changing at the Ganga ghat. Hues of pink, lavender, crimson and yellow took over the morning sky. A solitary launch anchored close-by was bathed in that crimson and golden glow. It took me back to the day when, sitting on the porch of my house in Goa, I had spotted a pair of hornbills feeding on wild berries in the tree across my porch. Soon, the couple was joined by another, and then another, till there were at least ten of them. The hornbills would visit me every few days. By sunset, they were joined by cuckoos, mynahs, egrets and other birds. There arose such a conversation amongst the birds that there was little else I could focus on. It reminded me of the Persian poet Farid ud-din Attar's long poem, 'The Conference of the Birds', where a group of 30 birds, led by a hoopoe, allegorically representing a Sufi master, leads his disciples to enlightenment.

I sensed someone was standing behind me at the ghat, and turned around to see Swapan-da. He lived close by, and was going about his morning chores when he saw me. His wife handed us cups of steaming hot black tea, and we began to talk. Swapan-da operated a launch, taking people into the forests, or to other islands; life behind the wheel was the only one he had known. As a child, he would accompany his father on the boat, one much smaller than the one he now owned. Swapan-da's father and uncle used to go into the forest to fish and collect firewood and honey, and sometimes, he was allowed to accompany them.

He proudly hinted he knew all the channels and creeks as well as he knew his own neighbourhood. 'I have sailed on them in my waking hours and when I have been asleep. You can never tell; sometimes the waters are so calm, and it is an amazing experience to travel through these mangroves which are a life-giving force to us. Yet, at other times, the same waters and mangroves can trick you into sailing right into the face of a disaster. It is all so unpredictable,' he told me.

Swapan-da was full of stories from the forest. Once, he,

along with his father, uncle and two neighbours were returning from the forest after spending three days there. The boat was loaded with the catch. The five of them were in the boat all throughout, and they bathed, cooked, ate and slept within the confines of the small boat, yet never felt constricted or uncomfortable. Swapan-da's father and the other men knew the safe spots to row to during *jwaar*, and where not to get stuck at the time of *bhaata*. 'It was almost like an in-built system in their psyche, and as a child, I was bewildered by the fact that they simply knew it all! As I have grown up, these things are no longer a mystery to me. I, too, know now. These forests are our providers and the rivers are our mothers: they give us all that we need. During that trip, the elders spread their nets and cast their fishing rods; they climbed trees to gather honey. Both processes require skill as well as patience. All the while, we kept uttering Bon Bibi's name, to keep us safe from the many perils one encounters in the forest. When it was time to leave, we rearranged everything neatly in the boat, and proceeded towards Bijaynagar.'

As they headed home, the sun began its descent and rain clouds began to gather at the farther end of the river. Not finding this unusual for that time of the year, nobody was overly concerned. As they picked up speed and made their way through narrow channels to emerge at Kalashdweep beach, they did not immediately realize that the breeze had also picked up speed. Only when they were closer to the beach and away from the protective cover of the mangroves did they realize that they were going to get caught in a storm. Going back into the forest was not an option at that point in time because the tide was about to change – they would have had to go much deeper inside the mangrove cover to be safe.

And then the storm was upon them – strong winds, immense roiling of the waters and a torrential downpour. Leaving the rowing to Swapan-da's father and uncle, the other two men set about creating a sail for the tiny boat, right there on the boat itself. After about ten minutes of hard work – braving the winds they cut out black plastic sheet, hoisted it up on a bamboo pole, and oriented it according to the direction of the wind to navigate them on their way – they were finally headed towards home. 'If we were closer to an island or its many embankments, we would have been alerted about the changing winds either by the urgent calls of the birds or by fellow boatmen. But since we were in the forest, we did not know of the impending dangers until they were upon us. And by then, it was impossible to do anything else except prepare the sail, sit tight, hold on, pray to Ma Bon Bibi and hope for deliverance.'

In the Sunderbans, Bon Bibi sends the *shushuk* – river dolphins – as her messengers. If you see them while on the rivers, it means that they are watching over you. It is the goddess' way of letting you know no harm will come to you.

'All through our ordeal, there was a pair of dolphins by our side, making an appearance beside our boat every few minutes. My uncle said that we would be fine because Ma had sent her messengers. And we reached the beach safely. I have grown up believing in these signs and I have been witness to such extraordinary things that I am scared of even mentioning them to people from the outside world. For example, very often, we see a rainbow around the moon. What can I tell tourists who stay overnight on a launch, anchored in the middle of a vast river in this forest of tides? Will they believe me if I say that Ma Bon Bibi is watching over us?'

Nowadays, Swapan-da takes tourists into the forest, where they gaze at and are amazed by the immensity of everything around them. But for Swapan-da, the Sunderbans and its wildlife and mangroves need to be preserved and protected, as both are quickly becoming extinct. 'We live without clean water and electricity; with almost no food and no doctor to go to when we are sick. These people come here with excitement to see the wonders of the mangrove forests, the rivers and the tides. They completely discount our existence. They forget that if it were not for us, it would be impossible for them to visit the Sunderbans. Who would take them into the forest, who would cook for them, take care of their needs while they are on the launch and busy taking photographs?' he asks.

The rainbow around the moon that Swapan-da mentioned is a phenomenon called halo or glory which happens when the moon passes through a very thin layer of clouds in the upper strata of the atmosphere. Its own light is refracted by the ice crystals in the clouds, thus creating a halo around it. Perhaps such phenomena are more pronounced in the wholesome and natural surroundings of the Sunderbans than in a city.

At times, lunar halos are an indication of approaching storms. Swapan-da and the others have learnt to read these signs, and their lives are ever so enriched by them.

Swapan-da's agony and sense of alienation from the world beyond the delta was understandable. We sat in silence for a few minutes, even as the *bayas* continued to chatter among the palm trees.

# Horizon

—

## Future of the Sunderbans

Palash did not turn up for work one morning. We got news that his wife had gone into labour the previous night and had delivered a baby boy in the wee hours of the morning. Over the course of the day, we kept getting updates on the newborn who, apparently, was underweight and was beginning to develop health complications. His tiny lungs were filling up with fluid and he was having trouble breathing. Of course, this diagnosis was made by the midwife who had helped deliver the baby, a village quack. By evening, the newborn was beginning to turn blue. Ultimately, we were given the terrible news that he didn't survive.

To everyone's surprise, Palash came to work the following day. He kept his head low and worked quietly through the day. Pain and disbelief were written all over his face. While 'grief' is usually personal, people in the Sunderbans have internalized it to such an extent that it borders on fatalism. Every aspect of their lives is intertwined with grief and, sadly, not much can be done about it. For instance, the frequent occurrence of cyclones. Even if the cyclones are not of an intensity enough to kill human beings, they cause considerable damage to their cultivable land, crops, livestock, boats or infrastructure such as jetties and embankments, and sometimes to all of these things. Then there are the wildlife attacks in the forests. Such is the fear among locals that they move around expecting each day to be their last. And such is the despondency that the women whose husbands go into the forests dress as widows until their husbands return safely.

Yet, even with this level of preparedness for the worst, how can one cope with the loss of a loved one, that too a child? How does one console the parent? I, too, was at a loss for words to convey to Palash how sorry I was. Words of condolence seemed so empty for a couple who had waited nine months for the baby to become a part of their lives, only to experience such short-lived happiness. I could not bring myself to say anything at all.

According to unofficial reports, nearly one-third of the babies that are born in the Sunderbans do not survive. Most childbirths take place at home and the lives of both the mother and the child are at great risk in the absence of proper medical facilities. In an effort to reduce the Infant Mortality Rate (IMR – number of deaths per 1,000 live births of children under one year of age), a news report in the *Business Standard* said that in mid-2016, the Trinamool Congress government decided to launch 'waiting hubs' for pregnant women on the islands of the Sunderbans.[1] The premise was that this would overcome the challenge of unsafe deliveries and ensure safe motherhood. Expectant mothers could come to these centres a few days before the delivery date and wait. Later, they would be shifted to a suitable hospital.

At the time of writing this book, these 'hubs' were few and far between. Perhaps due to the vastness of the region, it is practically impossible to have an outreach programme that benefits a substantial number of people. There have been some improvements, but not nearly enough. According to a December 2016 Sample Registration Survey, 'the IMR in 2011 was alarming – 32. In six years, the Mamata Banerjee-headed State Health Department has been able to reduce that to 26.'[2]

Infant mortality rate aside, young children in the Sunderbans are also prone to many common diseases due to malnutrition: common cold, flu, cough, diarrhoea, dental issues, etc. Factors like poverty, illiteracy, lifestyle, socio-cultural issues and lack of healthcare contribute greatly to children's ill health. Even women's health is a cause of major concern for the very same reasons. According to a news report in the *Economic Times*, in the Sunderbans, '...half the children suffer from malnutrition. Poor environmental conditions cause 3,800 premature deaths and 1.9 million cases of illness every year, primarily among children and adult women.'³

Those living in the delta attribute this to luck and karma. Over there, whether your child survives or not depends purely on your actions in your past life, for which you need to pay in your current lifetime. This human ability to simplify and categorize matters into convenient slots of karma baffles me.

Here was India in the 21st century: with a flourishing IT sector in Gurugram and Bengaluru, successful launch tests of the Agni IV missile, discoveries in medical science and regular inventions of new drugs. Yet, in complete contrast, newborns in the Sunderbans were dying because of lack of medical infrastructure.

But life goes on in this forest of tides. Amidst the grief we all felt for Palash's loss, there was some good news to be had. Molina, Jogesh-da's daughter and Prateet-da's wife, had given birth to a baby girl a few days ago. With the delivery being slightly premature, the mother and child were receiving the best possible care. Jogesh-da, the grandfather, was elated and couldn't stop smiling. However, Prateet-da, the father, was disappointed at his wife for having borne a baby girl again. Radhika, his first-born, now four years old, was also a girl. I was told he wasn't talking to Molina – a counter-intuitive way to express his disappointment. However, a stern talk by

Mayna, explaining that it was not Molina's doing and rather it was his own 'fault' that the baby was a girl, seemed to bring him around.

Life in the Sunderbans might be different from that in a city in terms of infrastructure and facilities. However, the notion of patriarchy remains the same. Whether it is an urban set-up or a region as remote as the forest of tides, the social system, in which a male holds the position of authority and makes decisions for the family, remains unchanged.

The hospital was to be readied for patients by November. Even if the functioning of the in-patient department was to get delayed – because we would have to obtain permissions and a license for that – the out-patient department (OPD) or clinics could function from the new building.

We were nearing the end of September and it was time to let go of the bottle-filling unit. Soon, the construction and all other work on the hospital building would come to an end. In this wilderness of the Sunderbans, the locals had come together to create for themselves a hope for a better future. Having been part of their journey, I learnt a crucial lesson: humility. I had also learned that no matter what, the people here would still live their lives amidst all the hardships. Life here would go on as naturally as the turning of the tides. Those who live close to nature perhaps have a certain acceptance of it because they respect the force which is so much greater than theirs: Mother Nature. In contrast, urban dwellers seem to think they have much more under their control.

I had come to the Sunderbans with my own dream: to build on that very hope that the locals had for their future. In return, I received acceptance and an all-encompassing love that knew no bounds. Not just from the people with whom I worked – Mayna, Jogesh-da, Panchu-da, Subroto, and everyone else who was a part of the Foundation's work team – but even from their families who adopted me like a child in need of care. I was guided at every step. I was taught the way of life in the Sunderbans: When to visit the forests and when to stay away; what to eat and how to eat it; and, most importantly, to live humbly, and to know that Mother Nature was going to provide for me, irrespective of come what may.

With a heavy heart, and a lot of gratitude, we broke the news to the women of our working group that, towards the month-end, we were going to stop filling the bottles. As with everything else, they took this information with their usual attitude of 'it's all part of life'. We had shared not just our working hours, but also intimacies of our respective lives. While sometimes those details were relatively significant, like news of our families and their well-being, the not-so-significant details were equally pertinent to our existence – like indulging in the vanity of having purchased a new saree or a set of new glass bangles.

Despite the lack of resources to ensure adequate meals each day, the women of the village had indulged me by sharing whatever little they cooked for their families. When the men went fishing, my share of the catch was always kept aside, cooked and delivered ready-to-eat. There was something about these people, who, despite limited resources, shared with all their heart.

One of the women from the bottle-filling unit, Sabita, was deaf and dumb. To my great delight, very early in our relationship itself, she and I had established that we did not need words to communicate. Sabita's deafness, and consequent muteness, was a handicap only for me. To her, this was not an issue. She went about her day as normally as anyone else. Before she came to work on the Foundation's campus, she cooked for herself, took her goats to graze and finished cleaning up the house. At the campus, she always arrived dressed in simple, cotton sarees.

I was told that her husband had died many years ago. Her two sons had grown up, gotten married, had their own children and had moved to nearby towns in search of livelihood opportunities. They visited Sabita at times. She had refused to go with them, insisting that she would continue her life in the way she knew best. Sabita's survival instinct was simple: she responded to each and every situation with a smile. Perhaps I was the one who was imagining how complex her life could be. I wondered how she would communicate if she ran into a problem. How would she express her emotions?

However, Sabita made me realize that one did not necessarily need words to convey something. What could be conveyed through the warmth of a hug or with the twinkle of an eye could never be compared to words. I was reminded of the Sufi mystic Rumi's words: 'Silence is the language of God; all else is poor translation.'

Durga Puja was almost upon us. We were to inaugurate the new building two days after the festival and we still had a lot of work to finish. The workers had decided that none of them was going to take time off during the celebrations. Instead, all they needed was to be let off a couple of hours early on that day to prepare for the big puja.

On behalf of the Foundation, Jogesh-da and Panchu-da visited the homes of every worker who had been a part of the construction team of the hospital and invited them to attend the inauguration ceremony with their entire family.

Once again, the panchayat felt left out and ignored. The Foundation had wanted to send an official letter of invitation to their office, and I would have asked Mayna to personally deliver it. But before this could be done, they came storming into our premises and started with their usual rant of the Foundation having cut down the mangroves. Some of us escorted them down to the embankment and showed them all the mangrove saplings newly planted along the periphery of the village. Moreover, we had carried out repairs along the embankment, at places where the tide waters had weakened its walls.

We told them that we simply could not afford to spend any more time with them as the hospital building had to be finished on time. After all, had the hospital been ready just a few weeks ago, Palash's baby would not have died. This silenced them. We invited them to the inauguration ceremony and informed them that Mayna would deliver a formal letter of invitation at their office. Everyone got back to work as there was no time to lose.

We were expecting the first lot of hospital equipment the following morning and there was a lot of preparation to be done. The monsoons were nearly over and there was only an occasional shower. The interiors of the hospital had almost been completed; we were now focusing our attention on the exterior – painting the walls and sprucing up the grounds around the building.

In a simple ceremony attended by the local people, government officials including forest officers, panchayat members and some of the volunteers of the Foundation who had come down especially for the event, the doors of the hospital building were opened for everyone.

We all left for Kolkata soon after, and the entire village gathered at the jetty to bid us adieu. The following day, I returned to Goa after eight long months. While I certainly needed the break, it also allowed me to step away from the project site and to think through the next steps. I would return to the Sunderbans to look into the functioning of the hospital, and other administrative issues.

Two weeks later, I went back to Bali with my daughter, Mallika, who was soon going to turn 13. She was anxious, yet excited and curious about experiencing a whole new way of living. She would learn things that one would skip in the formal set-up of a learning institution. Her school in Goa had allowed her to take a long break, provided she studied wherever she was and came back to take her exams. As a young child of four and five, Mallika had previously travelled with me to my projects in Kashmir and Gujarat, albeit only for a few days at a stretch. As I would realize later, this stint in the wonderland called the Sunderbans was to bring us even closer.

The fact that we were together for an uncertain period of time in a remote place where there were no avenues for social engagement, much less for any kind of entertainment, brought Mallika closer to nature. And she had no one else for company, except her mother. It was natural then for us to create our own little world within the world of mangroves.

Mallika immediately soaked in the new environment with ease. With great enthusiasm, she took to living with limited facilities, including electricity. She bravely adapted to a whole new lifestyle, which involved a different food culture. The fact that one couldn't just stroll across the street and buy daily supplies was at first amusing to her, but then she got used to the idea. She found it thrilling that there were no roads in the vicinity and one could only travel by boats.

Meanwhile, the Foundation had recruited some of the farmers-turned-labourers as non-medical workers for the hospital. A license had been applied for and advertisements were inserted in newspapers and journals for resident medical staff. Over the weeks, we were joined by a resident doctor, two nurses and an administrator. The medical clinic was now held three times a week, in the OPD wing of the hospital – exactly nine months after we first started work on the construction of the hospital building. Even though the hospital was not fully functional, people from nearby islands had begun visiting the OPD. They were no longer queuing up in the wee hours of the morning, secure in the knowledge that basic medical aid was now a regular part of their lives.

Mallika was witness to the disparity that has come to characterize modern India. On the one hand, there was the hospital building, the OPD clinic and the medical and non-medical staff, and on the other, quite in contrast, was the village life, complete with snakes and scorpions. Yet, she felt somewhat settled in her new surroundings. On one particular night, there was a heavy storm and a mini cyclone. The two of us sat by the window, watching the rain lash at everything. It was pitch dark outside, and the howling wind swept all around us. Every now and then, a flash of lightning would illuminate the surroundings in bright violet colour.

Mayna had been unable to return home after finishing the day's work because of the rainstorm. She joined us by the window and started recollecting events from the 2009 Aila cyclone, about how she, and everyone she knew, had climbed up on trees and watched as everything – their land, possessions, cattle, poultry and even people – got washed away.

Her favourite story was the one where, after a night full of chaos and destruction, everyone who survived simply fell asleep, still perched on the trees, exhausted beyond words. Mayna followed suit, but only after ensuring that her parents were all right on the next tree. And when she opened her eyes a few hours later, she saw a huge snake sharing her tree branch. The snake and Mayna looked into each other's eyes at the same instant; there was an instinctive, mutual understanding of the need to share the space and not harm each other. Both were equally scared, and unsure of whether they would survive the fury of the cyclone. As she recounted the incident, Mayna had a big smile on her face.

As we sat talking, the storm outside subsided. Though she did not expect or even hope for miracles, Mayna expressed the need for some relief in times of cyclones: for herself and all the local people. In the period after Aila, the state government had built a single cyclone shelter in the neighbourhood of Bijaynagar. It was not sufficient even for the number of people living in Bijaynagar, leave alone for Bali's entire population of 35,000. Subsequently, the Forest Department built another shelter. Whether these would be adequate in times of crises remained to be seen.

Mayna also wished there would be uninterrupted electricity and water supply for the people of the Sunderbans. At the same time, she expressed her anger at the local government for promising much during election campaigns, but not delivering on their promises.

Most locals here were dissatisfied with issues of governance, their primary concern being livelihood opportunities or the lack thereof. Some people are able to find work in their villages under the National Rural Employment Guarantee Act (NREGA), of building and repairing embankments or making brick roads. However, the opportunities and remuneration for the same are limited. Livelihood prospects still depend largely on the forest.

It is ironic that in the land of eighteen rivers, potable water is still not a guarantee; one has to struggle to access it. Women are more affected by this than men, since women are responsible for providing food and water for the family. With such limited resources, growing food in this largely agrarian society is also a challenge, due to lack of non-saline water for irrigation and the land not being suitable for growing a variety of crops. According to a news report in the *Economic Times*, '...more than two-thirds [of people in the Sunderbans] do not have access to safe water, and only 17% of the population are connected to the electricity grid, according to a 2014 World Bank report. ... A fifth of the population get only one meal a day and for a third of them, it is a sub-standard one.'[4] The report also states that half the population of the Sunderbans lives below the poverty line.

In such a scenario, it is hard to imagine a future for the delta and its people. As the islands are sinking, the local people themselves may not have enough space within the delta. The report adds, 'Between 1969 and 2009, the Sunderbans lost 210 sq. km of land and the future is not any brighter. About 250 sq. km of a previously productive zone will be lost in the next 5–10 years thanks to coastal erosion, cyclones and estuary changes, as per the World Bank report, which also says the annual cost of environmental damage could range from ₹344 crore to ₹1,065 crore.'[5]

Keeping such reports in mind, I wondered what the locals thought about their survival in the years to come. The Sunderbans is certainly becoming a popular tourism venue, both among Indians as well as foreigners, as more and more people crave quieter, less polluted areas for vacations. Would the forest of tides be able to sustain itself and its ever-growing population, with an increasing influx of tourists? While some locals, whose livelihoods are dependent on tourism – boat-owners, forest guides, guest house and resort owners – were happy about the growing tourism, others, especially old men and women, feared the loss of traditional values and respect for Mother Nature with the coming in of too many outsiders. Interestingly, when I spoke to a quack-doctor about this, he expressed his concern in no uncertain terms that with more people would come more awareness. I suspected that he feared that his livelihood was bound to be at risk!

Some people expressed what Swapan-da had already shared with me: that the people who came to visit the Sunderbans were mostly tourists and were not really concerned with the betterment of the region or its people. I sensed a deep bitterness as people spoke about their disappointment with the outside world, state and central governments included. They felt that the government simply did not care about them, which was why they were living in such abysmal conditions. At the same time, they also acknowledged that the Sunderbans was their home and an existence outside was unthinkable. Yes, the younger generation was going away to cities to study, and some of them would most likely stay there and find jobs that would pay them well. However, their roots were here and those could never be severed. Even if the children moved away, the elders of the family stayed here. And at the end of the day, the children would always come back to their families and the mangroves.

While things remained uncertain on the hospital license front, and the staff continued to feel isolated, we were ready to take our next step towards expanding the Foundation's medical outreach programme. It was decided that on Tuesdays, Wednesdays and Fridays, the hospital staff would travel to other islands to conduct mobile OPD clinics. Mondays, Thursdays and Saturdays were reserved for holding OPD clinics in the hospital premises. However, this led to a dilemma. Since we could not possibly reach out to all the inhabited islands – 102 in all, out of which 54 were inhabited – how were we to decide which islands were worse off than the others, and should, therefore, receive medical intervention? After visiting many islands, we chose to work on three.

Kumermarhi, close to the India–Bangladesh border, got its name from the large number of crocodiles in its vicinity (*kumir* in Bangla means crocodile). Since we were very close to the border, there was a marked presence of the Navy. The infrastructure on this relatively small island was supported by the presence of the armed forces and, therefore, the poverty in this place was not as stark as in others. Crocodile attacks and consequent deaths were regular occurrences, according to the people we met there. Someone from every other house in this place had suffered crocodile attacks, either while collecting tiger-prawn seed or while inside the forest, gathering resources.

The word remote did not do justice to Hemnagar village on Jogeshganj Island, the next one we had chosen, and which we visited a week after the 2015 Nepal earthquake. In Hemnagar, this earthquake was as normal a topic of conversation as the crop growing in people's fields once the tremors ceased. The shadows cast on their lives, homes and fields by the earthquake were apparent as cracks in the walls, as partially destroyed crops and the nervousness in simple conversations. The feeling of emptiness one got from the arid landscape that stretched brown and dry for miles was palpable and screamed abject poverty to us.

In Bali, when the earthquake struck, the ground beneath our feet had started trembling violently. The hospital building and the volunteers' home began to oscillate, and the water in the ponds started splashing, forcing the fish to jump out. It took a few seconds before it registered that we were experiencing the tremors of a massive earthquake.

At Hetalbari village on Mollakhali Island, our third site for the OPD, there were no jetties. Shanto, perhaps in his early twenties, helped anchor our boat along the village embankment. He was a distant cousin of Swapan-da, who, of course, was my guide and boatman during almost all my excursions in the forest of tides, including the visits to various islands. Shanto had recently returned to his village after a sojourn in Canning. He had left after cyclone Aila, unable to cope in the aftermath. However, spending a few years away from home doing odd jobs for a meagre income made him miss the familiarity of his land and the comfort of having a family to fall back on.

Shanto took us around the village to recce. The barrenness of the land was an indication of the aggression of nature. In

Shanto's words, the life of the people of Sunderbans was nothing but uncertain. The only certainty was that every time a cyclone visited them, it took everything away – money, food grains, meagre household items, poultry and animals, homes and even the pleasantness of an afternoon gossip session under a *tetul* tree. What remained was that all households were always ready for unannounced guests. You never knew who might turn up. The proverbial table was always set for extra people, without knowing who it might be. The empathy and inherent nature of sharing had survived many a cyclone in the Sunderbans.

More than the cyclones, which are termed as 'natural disasters', the Sunderbans is now under threat from 'man-made disasters'. Industrial waste from nearby towns and cities is released into rivers that merge with the sea. A WWF report says that domestic and industrial effluents and contaminated mud from dredging in Haldia, an industrial port town not far from Kolkata, are carried by tributaries to the Sunderbans, thereby adversely affecting its ecology. 'The Sunderbans delta has become susceptible to chemical pollutants such as heavy metals, organochlorine pesticides, polychlorinated biphenyls and polycyclic aromatic hydrocarbons which may have changed the estuary's geochemistry and affected the local coastal environment,' adds the report. [6]

There was news, in mid-2016, of two coal-fired power plants being set up in the Sunderbans. While one is a collaboration between India and Bangladesh, to strengthen bilateral relations, the other is an initiative of the Orion Group of companies in India. 'The most recently proposed project is the Orion power plant, a 630-megawatt plant being planned by the Orion Group. But the project receiving the most attention is the proposed Rampal power plant, which involves a partnership between India's state-owned National Thermal Power Corp. and the Bangladesh Power Development Board. The joint venture, which was established in 2012, is known as the Bangladesh–India Friendship Power Co. Ltd., or BIFPCL. The plan for the Rampal power plant is an installed capacity of 1,320 megawatts,' says a report by the *Washington Post*.[7]

If a power plant of such capacity does come up in the Sunderbans, it is bound to attract various industries to the area. For instance, a steady supply of electricity will be mandatory for the functioning of the plant, which, in turn will bring in more 'developmental projects' that could cause irreversible harm to the mangrove ecosystem. 'According to the National Oceanic and Atmospheric Administration, mangrove forests and coastal wetlands may be able to store up to five times more carbon than the same size tropical forest. Damaging these ecosystems can both harm their ability to continue storing carbon, as well as release carbon that's already sequestered,' adds the report.[8]

Moreover, during the transportation of coal through the intricate network of waterways of the Sunderbans, the likelihood of oil spills is high. The report furthers says, 'The region already experienced one such disaster two years ago, when an oil tanker collided with another vessel in the Shela River (in Bangladesh), spilling tens of thousands of gallons of oil into the water and threatening habitat for the rare Irrawaddy and Ganges dolphins and other wildlife in the area.'[9]

While such projects are likely to bring in economic and infrastructural 'development' and improve the quality of life by creating employment opportunities for the locals and bringing in facilities such medical aid, piped potable water and electricity, the end-result of such interventions is unpredictable. This is a rather tricky situation: choosing between continuing to let the locals live their lives in remoteness or introducing them to a life of facilities, but with the risk of damage to the splendour of Mother Nature and her resources. Is it possible to find a balance? And who is responsible for making the choice?

It had been close to two years since I had first arrived in the Sunderbans. Apart from the thrice-a-week OPD clinics at the hospital building on the Foundation's campus – which had been operational since November 2014 – it had now been approximately a year since the additional OPD clinics on the three islands were functional.

The work had kept me occupied all this time and I had been able to keep at bay the feelings associated with a posting in an outlying, inaccessible area. There was now a certain rhythm to the work which did not necessarily require my constant supervision or involvement. We were still awaiting the approval of the license of our hospital to operationalize the in-patient department. Simply put, this meant that we could not admit patients who needed long-term medical care into the hospital.

The remoteness of the place was also starting to take its toll on the medical staff. Not only were they feeling under-utilized, but also stranded, particularly due to lack of avenues for social engagement.

While I was debating the two issues – the future of the hospital and whether to continue living on the hospital campus – I couldn't help pondering over the larger question: was it practical to plan long-term for the region and its people, especially in the light of 'sinking islands'?

The School of Oceanographic Studies, Jadavpur University, had released a publication: *Mangrove Forest Cover Changes in Indian Sundarban (1986-2012) Using Remote Sensing and GIS*, according to which, from the year 1986 to 2012, 124.418 sq. km of mangrove forest cover has been lost. Prof. Hazra, head of the department, explained how climate change and the rise in the sea level had contributed to the phenomenon of the disappearing land, including mangrove forests in the Sunderbans, in the last part of the 21st century. 'This is because there is less fresh water flow and sediment supply in the western (Indian) part of the delta, so we have starvation of sediment and the rate of sea level rise is higher than sediment supply. Hence, we are losing land, including mangrove forest,' Professor Hazra told *The Hindu*.[10]

The impact of depletion of mangroves will directly reflect in the fishing trade. Joint secretary and project director of the Nature Environment and Wildlife Society (NEWS) NGO, Ajanta Dey, who has long been working in the Sunderbans, says, 'When fresh water inflow is missing, there is a change in mangrove succession and freshwater-loving species of mangroves are replaced by salt-water loving ones.' According to a news report in *The Hindu*, 'She [Ajanta Dey] said the immediate impact of salinity will be on the fishing community, where commercially sought after fish species will be replaced by fish that does not have as much market value.'[11]

What a vicious circle! Moreover, if the land was sinking, it also meant that there was less space for humans and wildlife to co-exist. What about the man-animal conflict then? Will it mean that both people and tigers, as well as other wildlife, were going to move away to 'greener pastures'? Or would they perish in the land of eighteen tides?

In 2014, in Sagara Island, there used to be a school near the embankment – Boatkhali Kadambini Primary School. In 2017, the school has disappeared. Tidal waters now reach beyond the area where the school building used to be. '...in the near future, all structures, agricultural lands, and the millions of residents all along India's 7,500 kilometre coastline will also be at heightened risk. The reason is that while sea level rise in the past has been caused primarily by warmer waters, it is now being fed increasingly by melting ice,' says a news report by *The Wire*.[12]

Wildlife attacks have been on a decline in the region, especially tiger attacks. Is it because of fewer tigers or more awareness amongst the locals? Perhaps both. Since the mention of the Bengal tiger is inseparable from the Sunderbans – whether in regard to conservation or attacks on humans – the two are often spoken of in the same breath. When I ponder over the prospects of tiger conservation in the delta, I wonder how the locals feel about the fact that, at times, tigers get more attention than them.

The tigers seem to be safe from the threat of extinction, at least for now, when one considers the results of all the conservation projects for both conserving tigers and creating awareness among the locals about the wild beast. 'While the Bengal tiger is also endangered, as per the government's latest tiger estimation, the Sunderbans had 76 of them in 2014 compared to 70 in 2010. Sunderbans has been lauded for its tiger conservation efforts.'[13]

The tiger, apart from being feared by all, commands a certain sense of awe and respect, which has also helped the cause of conservation. Perhaps a non-conflicting co-existence is possible, if both man and animal live within their respective territories and humans learn to respect the boundaries. And if tourism is conducted responsibly, in a way that it does not put undue pressure on the ecology of the forest of tides.

After spending nearly two years in the delta, to choose between withdrawing from the project or continuing to live on the Foundation's campus on Bali Island was difficult. While I knew that my moving on would affect the project, I was equally conscious of the toll it was taking on me. I invoked Bon Bibi for guidance and thought of her own dilemma. On the one hand, she had saved Dukhe from his uncles' treachery and from Dakshin Rai, adopting the demon-god as her son. On the other hand, she had defeated Dakshin Rai's mother, Narayani, in war, but forgiven them both and granted them the boon of life. While Dukhe represented humans, Dakshin Rai represented the tigers and the realm of forests. How would Bon Bibi balance this delicate relationship? And if she ever needed to choose between either, whose side would she take?

# EPILOGUE

Mallika and I returned to Goa towards the end of 2015.

The hospital was granted a license sometime in mid-2016. After my return, the OPD clinics, both on Bali Island and the other islands, continued to function for a few months without a resident volunteer. Perhaps inevitably, the mobile clinics had to halt operations due to inadequate infrastructure. The clinics on Bali, now reduced to twice a week, continued. They were managed by a team of doctors from Kolkata, since the resident medical staff had quit, unable to cope with where they were required to live.

I could understand their apprehensions and inconveniences. Apart from the lack of choice in food and the complete absence of any kind of social life, the long, risky and uncomfortable commutes troubled them – both with respect to time as well as the nature of transportation – not just to visit their families, but also to the remote islands that the Foundation wanted to reach out to.

In the interim, the panchayat, finding the ground clear, started creating trouble yet again. They garnered support from those who had been denied the opportunity to work on the construction of the hospital. These locals, with very strong backing from the panchayat, insisted that the Foundation should hire them. It was impossible and impractical because they demanded technical jobs that required semi-skilled or skilled workers, which they were not. Unfortunately, the non-medical staff who had built the hospital had to leave their jobs, as the panchayat played its power cards again.

Meanwhile, Mother Nature, too, had a plan in place. The push and pull of the tides results in continuous shifting of the land across the delta. As a result, any building – whether a straw-and-mud *kachha* structure or a steel-and-cement *pucca* structure – requires constant maintenance. Unfortunately, the hospital had no one to look after it.

The state government was well aware of the construction of the Samarpan Charitable Hospital. While the Foundation did not seek active help from the government during the construction phase, its support was solicited when the license was applied for. The long process and unnecessary trouble that the Foundation was put through before the license was issued had made us wary of approaching the state government for any further assistance. The government didn't extend its support either. Currently, the hospital, its building and the jetty are being managed interminably, at best, long distance, and at a huge cost.

While the Foundation put in its best effort to bring about a change for the better in the lives of the local people of the Sunderbans, the efforts did not really bear fruit. What this meant for the Foundation is one part of the story. The more crucial and relevant part is the loss of hope for the local people – those who built the hospital and those who would have benefitted as a result of it. However, the Universe has its own individual relation with each one of us. What it chooses to teach us, and how, is a matter of speculation.

Mayna continues to be employed by the Foundation. She is involved in the daily affairs of its existence on Bali Island, no matter how trivial. She carries on with her own personal form of advocacy, by being part of various groups that strive for the betterment of the forest of tides and its people. Jogesh-da has gone back to being the farmer. His son, Subroto, the carpenter, is always there for people, beyond the call of duty, as it were.

Sabita spends her time with her goats and chasing away children who come into her courtyard to steal fruit from her cheeku and *tetul* trees. Prateet-da is inseparable from his two daughters. Swapan-da ferries tourists from Godkhali and takes them for visits into the forest, all the while bewitching them with his endless stories.

It is believed that if one brings back fruit or saplings from the forest of mangroves, the fruit turns bitter and the saplings grow into weak trees that bear tasteless fruit. No animals from the forest are to be brought back either. Owning a piece of land in the forest is out of the question. And when one goes into the forest, it is necessary to finish all the cooked food in the house before leaving. This is to prevent people from consuming fruit from the forest because they will not be hungry. Moreover, going into the forest with unfinished food at home is a sign of having enough resources, in which case going there is rather inappropriate. One is supposed to go to the forest empty-handed, with a pure heart, leaving aside all hierarchies and divisions of caste and religion. Of course, littering, defecating and throwing garbage either in the forest or in its rivers is considered disrespectful. This proscription is followed strictly; the locals caution their children and launch drivers mention this as a rule to the tourists who come to visit the mangrove forests.

Here in the forest of tides, Mother Nature is both bountiful as well as devastating. She completely envelops the lives of those who live here. The people, in turn, follow the rituals of the forest and believe in their powers as much as in the forces of the forest itself. Therefore, the forest gods and goddesses are not to be invoked frivolously; like the waters, they can preserve or destroy. The spirits of the forest are omnipresent and observe everything. No one walks into the forest on a full moon night or on a new moon night, or on Fridays. No one turns around when they hear a voice calling out their names in the forest. Who knows...it could be the evil powers at work.

Since the lives of the people are inseparable from the forest, they have developed their own cult of syncretism where Hindus, Muslims, the tribals and everyone else comes together to worship their own set of gods and goddesses along with revering snakes, tigers, crocodiles, fish, the mangroves and even their boats. When honey-gatherers come together to go to the forest, they first worship their boats, tying a piece of red cloth to it, which is symbolic of the boat being sacred. They also blow horns very loudly before entering the forest, announcing their arrival and thereby seeking permission from the powers that be. When they locate a beehive, they smoke up the entire area to get rid of the bees and then the first piece of the hive is offered to Bon Bibi. In an act of sheer humility, women whose men go into the forest choose to dress up as widows, almost begging fate to protect their men from the dangers of the wild.

The Sunderbans – mystical, majestic and equally mysterious – a land like no other.

When I had first arrived in the Sunderbans, my maiden encounter with the creatures of the mangrove forests happened soon enough. A pair of Russell's vipers – a species of highly venomous snakes – were courting each other in the Foundation's courtyard. In an act of catch-me-if-you-can, the female was playing hard-to-get as the male slithered and wrapped its body around her. Continuing the game, the duo created quite a performance – the female escaping and the male chasing – all across the campus.

I was mesmerized by the sheer spectacle of their courtship. When the couple reached the fencing of the campus, the female easily navigated her way through the barbed wire, but the male, being thicker, got stuck. It tried hard to negotiate its way out, but despite its slippery body, it was unable to slip past. The piercing wires and the scorching heat of the sun irritated the male no end. Angrily, it flayed its body over and over again, but in vain. The female, meanwhile, vanished into the nearby mangroves.

After about half-an-hour later, when it still lay there helpless, and not-so-angry, Guru-da, the campus guard, quietly snipped at the barbed wire with a pair of nose pliers, setting the snake free, for a fresh lease of life. It was almost like a rebirth for the Russell's viper. What and how would the snake have felt on being able to break free? Perhaps like a butterfly breaking out of its chrysalis, seeing the world anew after being released from its self-built cage.

I was reminded of this incident as Mallika and I were leaving the Sunderbans. While we weren't exactly breaking free from captivity, we were going back to a 'regular' world after having lived in the forest of tides, at best described as other-worldly. We were armed with the lived experiences of this other world, and would carry its magic and mysticism into the more mundane world…seeking the Divine everywhere and looking for hidden messages within the most ordinary.

# MY BON BIBI

The sweat we hold in the clasp of our hands
bears the history of an emotion
that can be expressed only in shared breath

> In that shade, the sun is the absent king
> In that shade, the sun is present as death
> What it gives life to, it shall also burn

I float on you, earth dancing on water
To feel water, grasp the certitude of earth
that manifests as peaks of ice, sun-melt rivers
furrowing the crevices of tilled land

I'm making my way into your forested land
of eighteen tides, with moons fuller than your eyes

Our futures are a journey into pasts
We inhabit absences in each other
We are the presence that can be felt, not touched
We are the reflection of sky in water

*(11 January 2015)*

S. Anand

# NOTES

## Preface

[1] Pandey, Jhimli Mukherjee, 'Sundarbans habitation dates to 3BC', *Times of India*, 30 October 2013.

[2] Sahgal, Bittu, Sumit Sen and Bikram Grewal, *The Sundarbans Inheritence*, Mumbai: Sanctuary Asia, 2007.

## Land

[1] Sahgal, Bittu, Sumit Sen and Bikram Grewal, *The Sundarbans Inheritence*, Mumbai: Sanctuary Asia, 2007.

[2] *Wild Tiger Estimation of Tiger Census- 2010*, Ministry of Environment, Forest and Climate Change, Government of India, 2011.

[3] Sahgal, Bittu, Sumit Sen and Bikram Grewal, *The Sundarbans Inheritence*, Mumbai: Sanctuary Asia, 2007.

[4] Jalais, Annu, *People and Tigers: An Anthropological Study of the Sundarbans of West Bengal, India*, PhD Thesis, London: London School of Economics and Political Science, University of London, 2004.

[5] http://www.sundarbans.org

[6]    Montgomery, S.Y., 'Why do the tigers of Sundarbans eat humans when tigers around the world seldom do?', *Scroll*, 8 September 2016.

[7]    Sahgal, Bittu, Sumit Sen and Bikram Grewal, *The Sundarbans Inheritence*, Mumbai: Sanctuary Asia, 2007.

[8]    http://www.ramsar.org

[9]    http://whc.unesco.org/en/list/798

[10]    Ghosh, Dipanjan and Sreeparna Ghosh, 'Sunderban Mangroves: Challenges to Survival', *Science Reporter*, February 2013.

[11]    Jalais, Annu, *People and Tigers: An Anthropological Study of the Sundarbans of West Bengal, India*, PhD Thesis, London: London School of Economics and Political Science, University of London, 2004.

[12]    Ibid.

## Water

[1]    http://wbplan.gov.in/HumanDev/DHDR/24%20pgsSouth/Chapter%2009.pdf

[2]    Roy, Atul Chandra, *The Career of Mir Jafar Khan (1757–65 A.D.)*, Calcutta: Das Gupta, 1953.

[3]    http://sundarbanforest.com/history-%20of-sundarban/

[4]    Sahgal, Bittu, Sumit Sen and Bikram Grewal, *The Sundarbans Inheritence*, Mumbai: Sanctuary Asia, 2007.

[5]    Bhaumik, Subir, 'Fear rise for sinking Sundarbans', BBC UK, 15 September 2003.

[6]    'Rising sea levels and tidal erosion eating up Sunderbans', Downtoearth.org, 7 June 2015.

[7]  Mukherjee, Sanhita, 'The Sinking Sundarbans: But How Will the Government Correct its Own Folly?', *Mainstream Weekly* VOL LIV No 15, 2 April 2016.

[8]  Singh, Shiv Sahay, 'Sinking Sunderbans islands no poll issue', *The Hindu*, 10 May 2014.

## Mangroves

[1]  Ghosh, Dipanjan and Sreeparna Ghosh, 'Sunderban Mangroves: Challenges to Survival', *Science Reporter*, February 2013.

[2]  Jalais, Annu, *People and Tigers: An Anthropological Study of the Sundarbans of West Bengal, India*, PhD Thesis, London: London School of Economics and Political Science, University of London, 2004.

[3]  Jalais, Annu, 'Bonbibi: Bridging Worlds', *Indian Folklife*, National Folklore Support Centre, January 2008.

## Horizon

[1]  'Waiting Hubs for Pregnant Women in Sundarbans: Mamata', *Business Standard*, 27 June 2016.

[2]  'Bengal Second in India in reducing Infant Mortality Rate', All India Trinamool Congress, Aitofficial.org, 10 July 2017.

[3]  Seetharaman, G., 'Why climate change and pollution threats to the Sundarbans cannot be taken lightly by governments', *Economic Times*, 19 April 2015.

[4]  Ibid.

[5]  Ibid.

[6]  Ibid.

7   Harvey, Chelsea, 'A new power plant could devastate the world's largest mangrove forest', *Washington Post*, 18 July 2016.

8   Ibid.

9   Ibid.

10  Singh, Shiv Sahay, 'Cimate change impact: Sunderbans steadily losing its famed mangroves', *The Hindu*, 1 July 2017.

11  Ibid.

12  Adve, Nagraj, 'What a School in Bangal Teaches Us About Sea Level Rise', *The Wire*, 9 December 2017.

13  Seetharaman, G., 'Why climate change and pollution threats to the Sundarbans cannot be taken lightly by governments', *Economic Times*, 19 April 2015.

# ACKNOWLEDGEMENTS

This book is ever so enriched by its association with Patrick, my mentor, for whose continued guidance I am grateful.

During my work at the Sunderbans, Mallika transformed from daughter to friend. The Samarpan team indulged me, as always. A special mention of the Kolkata team who not just helped out with the various aspects of the project but also took immense care of me. Thank you to all those who worked behind the scenes and gave generously of their time and resources, to make the project happen.

The local team of people from within the Sunderbans, who worked relentlessly to put together the building of the hospital, ought to know that they have created history. During such time, support provided by the Nature Club and the Wildlife Protection Society of India, the Bijaynagar panchayat, the Forest Department of the Sunderbans Tiger Reserve and Biosphere Reserve, has been invaluable.

Without Amish, this book would never have been born; I am appreciative of his encouragement. Anand, my confidant, put things in perspective and also penned two lovely poems especially for this book. A special 'thank you' to all those who came and lived with me during the various phases of construction, including my mother and my niece.

A big 'thank you' to Hachette India for putting their faith in me, yet again. Poulomi Chatterjee made sure that I didn't give up; Sohini Pal read through various drafts of the book, and Ansila Thomas fine-tuned all the last-minute issues. Thank you, Maithili Doshi Aphale of Studio Em+En, for the splendid cover and thank you, Arushi Pareek, for a thorough proofing of the text.